Christina Hedin, Sophie Kauper, Karl Stocker (Eds.)

Lessons On Change

15 Creative Minds Share Their Stories

Birkhäuser
Basel

Table Of Contents

| 4–9 | **Lessons On Change. An Introduction** |
| | Christina Hedin, Sophie Kauper, Karl Stocker |

| 10–25 | **Designers Can Show What Positive Change Looks Like** |
| | Stuart Walker |

| 26–37 | **Creating A Design Manual** |
| | Lilián González-González |

| 38–53 | **Swimming In A River Of Change** |
| | Gunnar Rundgren |

| 54–65 | **Art As Tool For Emancipation** |
| | Stella Rollig |

| 66–77 | **Design And Complexity** |
| | Pier Paolo Peruccio |

| 78–97 | **Detroit—Invisibility In The Magnificent City** |
| | Marsha Music |

| 98–105 | **Film Can Say Everything At Once** |
| | Lukáš Berberich |

106–129	**Creating Something New Because There Is No Solution**
	Barbara Meyer
130–141	**Does Fear Stand In The Way Of Change?**
	Ola Fransson
142–157	**We Need To Ask The Right Questions**
	Julia Kloiber
158–169	**Commuter In A Communicating World**
	Andy Kaltenbrunner
170–181	**Empowering Change Through Design Education**
	Sigrid Bürstmayr, Bettina Gjecaj
182–193	**Curiosity And Creativity**
	John Howkins
194–203	**Youth Involvement As A Catalyst For Change**
	Carlotta Beghi

Words by Christina Hedin, Sophie Kauper, Karl Stocker

Lessons On Change.
An Introduction

The world is changing rapidly. Some of these changes improve our lives, for example we can use our phones to read the news or communicate with friends and family. Now, we do not have to wait weeks for a letter to arrive. Far too quickly, we tend to get used to the fast pace of our constantly developing environment and the never-ending stream of innovative technology. Tech that had just been introduced is soon destined for oblivion.

Always being told about the great advantages of this fast-paced development, and growing up regarding our world as this remarkable and unique place, one might wonder what fuels ongoing wars, why do we exceed our planetary boundaries and how is it possible that poverty is still an issue in almost every country to this day, despite millions of people overcoming financial hardship.

These are all alarming reports that, ideally, we should not have to deal with anymore given our economic, social, and technological advancements in recent years. Many of these problems have been forgotten about, mostly because the media in the Global North has never put a focus on them. The conflict in the Congo and women struggling in Afghanistan are all still pretty real and happening as we speak. Not many people are aware of the current situation in high-risk areas that are not cutting the front page anymore.

Climate change The evidence for climate change is overwhelming. All around the globe, we can already see its consequences, including flooding, fires, and other types of extreme climatic aberrations. Floods have become so common that many severe events are no longer reported globally. The effects of global warming are occurring much faster than scientists had predicted.

Despite this, we remain reluctant to transform society in a more sustainable way. A minority of companies and states actively try to stop the transition to a fossil-free world, persuading individuals, governments, and businesses to continue relying on non-renewable energy sources. The vast majority of countries and companies, however, acknowledge climate change but still fail to take significant action. The societal changes required to delay its progression are immense and must involve every facet.

The pandemic showed us that a quick change in society is possible. So why do we not respond to the climate crisis with the same urgency?

War In Sweden and other countries, the focus has shifted to military rearmament due to the war in Ukraine. The Swedish government wants to be prepared for a potential war and is allocating enormous amounts of money to militarization but neglects to invest a similar level of resources into addressing the climate crisis.

Rich and poor The world has been flooded by millionaires in pursuit of adventures involving fancy hotels, luxury yachts and private jets. "Existing products and practices are freely discarded in favor of the latest fashions, the most up-to-date devices. Such extravagant lifestyles expose the fact that we do not value material things; we value newness, and the environmental toll is immense." (Stuart Walker, Design for Resilience: Making the Future We Leave Behind, MIT Press 2023, p. 1).

Hunger and hardship However, the distribution of wealth seems to be a harder challenge to solve. We still have one billion people who go to bed hungry every night, while another billion struggle with obesity.

The future is digital It can no longer be overlooked—the future is digital. Between dystopian fear of technology and utopian enthusiasm for it, all kinds of imagination currently exist in public discourse, finding expression everywhere. Scientists, designers, and artists have begun analyzing, illustrating, and commenting on the prevailing dominance of bits and machines. They examine the profound changes currently reshaping our lives. Yet, even after millions of years of human life and evolution, we remain rooted in our sensory experiences—what we can feel, smell, see, and hear. (Kunstforum 265, Digital. Virtuell. Posthuman?)

Hope In this world of crises, we also see determination—people who truly make a tremendous change and influence others, either on a personal level or in their workplaces. In moments of crisis or catastrophe, individuals extend support to others in generous ways.

We have the power The change that we need in society is driven by people—clever and brave individuals with a deep knowledge in their fields. People who see creativity as a tool for development and who gather others eager to join their mission. By working together, we can discover new ways to develop the world today.

To better understand the change required in this world, the editors of this book, Christina Hedin, and Karl Stocker, invited some of the people in their network to write articles about change and how they have been working with development in their respective fields. Sophie Kauper, the third editor, together with Lauren Brooks, is responsible for the translations as well as the linguistic and editorial processing of the diverse texts.

The contributors The authors featured in this book live in different countries and are experts in various fields, but all of them have made a change in their respective domain. They have come up with innovative ideas and implemented them to a broader audience.

What they have in common is their awareness of the world's challenges. However, instead of succumbing to despair, they work consistently and humbly to improve the world with their own expertise.

Our book begins with Stuart Walker, who, in his interview Designers Can Show What Positive Change Looks Like, reflects on his career path. As a former engineer in the oil industry focused on maximum extraction, he later transitioned to art and design. Today, he works as a designer, university teacher, and author. What fascinated him most was the power of designers to envision a better future. Design can not only enrich aesthetically but also serve as a bridge to open people up to positive changes.

Lilián González-González, industrial designer and Academic Coordinator at the Anáhuac University of Mexico, describes in Creating A Design Manual the development of a guide aimed at equipping students and professionals to address complex social challenges and conflicts in marginalized contexts while fostering hope. The manual integrates insights from various fields of knowledge such as critical theory, philosophy, art, literature, linguistics, and other humanities and social science areas to enable a design practice with transformative, symbolic, disruptive, and instituting power. The text concludes with a call to extend the principles of the manual beyond the academic realm to allow for broader application in professional and collaborative practices in social design.

Gunnar Rundgren tells his story in Swimming In A River of Change. He is one of the pioneers of organic agriculture in Sweden, and in the article, he describes how it all started on a self-sufficient collective farm. Over the years, the farm developed, leading to collaboration with other farmers and the establishment of the first organic marketing cooperative in Europe, which eventually resulted in the creation of organic certification in Sweden. After the development of the organic sector in Sweden, Gunnar continued to advance this movement in several other countries. The article also describes why Gunnar started to write books and it ends with his analysis on society today, including how capitalism can be harmful, how we see nature, and our obsession with setting goals.

Stella Rollig reflects in her interview titled Art as Tool for Emancipation, on her path to the world of art and her roles as a curator and, currently as the General Director of the Belvedere in Vienna. She emphasizes the importance of art as an instrument of emancipation and highlights the function of the museum in preserving and contextualizing cultural heritage. She discusses the current challenges for museums, including global orientation and sustainability. Lastly, she expresses optimism in light of the growing social awareness in the younger generation of museum professionals.

Pier Paolo Peruccio, Professor at the Politecnico di Milano, starts his text, Design And Complexity, by exploring the multifaceted nature of the term design, acknowledging its diverse interpretations, and emphasizing its continuous and pervasive influence on our actions and decisions. Furthermore, the article delves into the concept of complexity, highlighting its interconnected and systemic nature, especially in addressing contemporary crises. It underlines the value of systems thinking in understanding the intricate relationships within systems and how this approach is instrumental in tackling complex issues. Finally, the article provides insight into the Archeology in Transit project, which uses artifacts as a key lens to understand migration intricacies, illustrating the significant role of design and research in addressing global issues.

Marsha Music, author and cultural historian, describes in Detroit, The Magnificent City her experiences and observations of Detroit's history, culture, and evolution. She shares her family's connection to the city, including her father's role as a record producer and their experiences in different neighborhoods. Marsha delineates the demographic shifts and the impact of urban renewal and various crises, such as the 1967 Rebellion and subsequent upheavals, on the city and her family. Moreover, she addresses the evolving social dynamics, economic changes, and the intersection of race and visibility in Detroit. Marsha emphasizes the need for a more inclusive and accurate portrayal of the city's history, culture, and the contributions of its Black residents. Overall, the text provides a comprehensive insight into the multifaceted history, challenges, and promising developments in Detroit, as observed and experienced by Marsha Music.

Lukáš Berberich's contribution Film Can Say Everything At Once, describes the activities of Kino Úsmev, which he leads, aiming to not only be a cinema but also a place for dialogue, diversity, and political engagement. Lukáš sees his work as a contribution to change in society, with values such as inclusivity and openness playing a central role. Despite various challenges, such as inadequate financial support, positive feedback and international recognition of his project motivate him.

Barbara Meyer reflects in Creating Something New Because There Is No Solution on her diverse professional experiences and how she was influenced by her time in the mountain region of Switzerland and her work at the cultural center Schlesische27 in Berlin. Barbara expresses her views on the necessity of using artistic strategies in various social areas to promote transformations. Her commitment to creating an alternative educational landscape as well as the integrative work with refugees and migrants expresses her vision of a diverse and open society.

Ola Fransson reflects about change and our human nature in the article Does Fear Stand In The Way of Change? He asks why humanity remains inert, inactive, and unshaken despite being aware of today's insights about climate change, especially in the wake of an increasing number of environmental disasters. Is it possible to find answers by exploring our cultural heritage and traditional knowledge? Meeting all kinds of people in his line of work, he realized how differently nature is observed and perceived. To show these contrasts and variances, Ola curated an exhibition with thoughtful design elements to showcase the diverse perspectives. By understanding and acknowledging these varying views of nature, Ola believes we can initiate a crucial conversation about where we stand and where we are going.

Julia Kloiber's interview titled We Need To Ask The Right Questions explores her personal journey, professional development, and current sociopolitical engagement, particularly in the context of digitalization through her work with the non-profit organization SUPERRR Lab. She emphasizes the importance of collaboration, networking, and fostering open dialogues to drive social and political change. The interview also discusses specific projects focused on improving working conditions for content moderators and researching human rights violations in the digital supply chain.

Andy Kaltenbrunner, university lecturer, journalist, and founder of the Medienhaus Wien, explains his efforts to invigorate media education and support journalism in Austria and other countries in his interview, Commuter In A Communicating World. He emphasizes the vital role of social mobility, education, and ethical responsibility in relation to societal development. The interview also explores topics such as artificial intelligence, technological development, and their societal impacts. Lastly, Kaltenbrunner articulates his hope for a better future through the promotion of critical thinking, social responsibility, and a diverse, globally oriented generation of young people.

Sigrid Bürstmayr and Bettina Gjecaj, both lecturers at the Institute of Design and Communication at the University of Applied Sciences in Graz, discuss the future of design theory in their dialogue titled Empowering Change Through Design Education. They engage in dialogue about topics like social and ecological design and reflect on their personal backgrounds and experiences that have sparked their interest in sustainability. The conversation emphasizes the significance of sustainable design across various disciplines and describes how designers can build bridges between social groups. Furthermore, they address the responsibility regarding ecological, economic, and social sustainability, and how these principles can be integrated into design education.

John Howkins, a writer, professor, and entrepreneur, reflects in his article Curiosity And Creativity, on what he has been focusing on in the last years—ingenuity and innovation. He sees that creativity can give fresh solutions to the problems that threaten our survival, such as climate change, poverty, and conflicts. The other word in the title, curiosity, was the driving force for John to go to China. That first trip has now been followed by many, and in the interview, he describes how he became part of the creative industry development in China.

Carlotta Beghi gives a glimpse of Parma, the world-famous City of Gastronomy, in the article Youth Involvement As A Catalyst For Change. Carlotta describes the potential and benefits of investing in youth skills but she also describes the challenges involved in making it happen. As the Focal Point for Parma's UNESCO designation as a Creative City of Gastronomy, she has been instrumental in developing the city's recognition for ten years.

Modesty Modesty is perhaps the quality that applies to all our authors. The process and the results are important to them, so this gives them the opportunity to pursue their respective paths consistently and unwaveringly. The focus is on change, not on marketing themselves. Let us conclude this introduction with a quote from Annie Lennox, who has been advocating for human rights, feminism, the fight against poverty, and AIDS awareness for decades: "Once you're an activist, you don't think about it; it just becomes part of you, a job that you do every day. It's not like I just fall from the sky and do something now and then. It's not a performance; it's a deep, deep commitment on my part." (Kurier, 25.12.2024, p. 36)

We hope that the articles inspire new ideas and meaningful change.

CHRISTINA HEDIN, SOPHIE KAUPER, KARL STOCKER

A conversation between   Stuart Walker   & Karl Stocker

Designers Can Show What *Positive Change Looks Like*

STUART WALKER is Chair of Design for Sustainability at the Manchester School of Art at the Manchester Metropolitan University. He is also Emeritus Professor, co-founder and Director of the Imagination Research Centre at Lancaster University; Emeritus Professor at the University of Calgary, Canada, where he served as Director of Industrial Design, Associate Dean Academic and Associate Dean Research. He is also Visiting Professor of Sustainable Design at Kingston University, London. His research in design for sustainability has been published and exhibited internationally, and his many books include Sustainable by Design; Design Realities; and Design & Spirituality. His latest book, Design for Resilience, is published by The MIT Press.

K S **What was the trigger for you to get involved with design and think about design?**

S W   Well, it was, in many ways, a progression. I started out, as I think you may know, as an engineer. I was a petroleum engineer in the Middle East.

As a teenager, I worked in the steelworks in my hometown. It was a steel and mining town. Later, I studied Mining Engineering, and I worked in the mining industry. And then I joined a major oil company, working in the Middle East, the Netherlands and London. I saw the impacts of large-scale industry and what it was doing to the world. But also, all that time I was working as a professional engineer I had a hankering towards art and design.

Long before this, when I was at school, I was reasonably good at art and woodwork. But my parents wanted me to be more academic, so I was persuaded to drop those hands-on, skills-based creative subjects and instead pursue the sciences like physics, biology, maths and chemistry, and the subjects I was not so good at or interested in. But I did them and I did them fairly well. Later, in my last years of school, I studied geology, and this led to university and a degree in Mining Engineering, and so this was the direction I was taking. I completed my PhD in Mining Engineering, and I became a petroleum engineer. I worked in the industry for seven or eight years. But after that time, I just felt I could not keep doing it. First of all, I was not really interested in the work, and secondly, I was becoming increasingly aware of the damage it was causing to the natural environment. But these environmental consequences did not seem to be of much interest to the industry at that time. I am not sure they are even now. I do not see them thinking about doing things very differently. There is no real commitment by the oil majors to transition towards clean energy.

One of the turning points in my thinking was when I was out on an exploration well in the southern desert of the Saudi peninsula. I was the petroleum engineer on the rig, whereas most of the others were contracted drilling crew. They just 'turn to the right and make hole' - that is their job. There's one petroleum engineer on the rig to monitor what is going on. He analyses the drilling fluids, taking and analysing geological samples from the rock we are drilling through, supervising wireline-logging contractors and so on. Then, when the drill reaches a certain depth, we would call in other contractors, Schlumberger wireline and, sometimes, drill-stem testers who set up and try to flow the well, to confirm if there is producible oil there. So, I was on this well, and it was a long way from anywhere. And we got down to the formation and did the wireline logging. The analysis indicated an oil-bearing formation.

We decided to do a drill-stem test, which temporarily produces the well through the drill string, and in this case, it flowed at about 400 barrels a day, so it was a good well. However, the nearest production station was some distance away and it was going to take around two weeks to lay a pipeline from there to the well. So, all this was great, and everybody was happy that it was such a promising well.

But then I was woken in my portacabin at the rig in the early hours of the morning. Headlights were shining in through the window and I could hear trucks moving.

I quickly got dressed and went out to have a look, and there were all these tanker trucks arriving. And I asked what was going on. I was told that the main office at the coast had decided to start producing the well right away into the tanker trucks, which would then take it to the production station. So, until the pipeline was laid, there was going to be a continual convoy of tanker trucks coming and going from the well to the production station.

It was only going to take two weeks till the pipeline arrived, so I asked, "What's the rush? This seems crazy. This oil has been in the ground for millions of years. We've only just discovered it and it's a precious resource. Why do we have to produce it to the trucks? Why don't we just wait two weeks for the pipeline to arrive?" Nobody at the rig could give me a good answer, so, when I got back to the office on the coast, I continued to ask and was told that I should go talk to the economist. So, I went to talk to the economist and asked him what it was all about. Why the rush? He went through the figures and showed me that the oil produced in these two weeks, if it is not produced now, will only be recovered right at the end of the well's life. And so, it is much more profitable to produce it now than it is at the end. It was a purely economic argument. There was no consideration given to the preciousness of these natural resources, nor to waiting and treating it in a more respectful, conservational way. No consideration of subsequent generations.

> "It was just a case of *produce, produce, produce,* as fast as possible. And then sell it as fast as possible."

It suddenly dawned on me that this is how we are looking at the whole of the Earth. This is how we are looking at our home, we are drilling it, digging into it, tearing it all up in quarries and mines and producing, producing, producing as fast as possible for maximum profit. This is what all these extractive industries are doing, and this is what I was part of and contributing to. And it is all feeding the growth-based economy of more, more, more. We constantly want growth, so we endlessly produce more and more stuff. And then we throw it away and we replace it because there's always a new model. And it suddenly just seemed crazy to me. What are we doing? Where are we trying to get to? What are we trying to achieve? What point are we trying to reach? Of course, nobody ever asked these kinds of questions. Nobody ever asked "Why?"

So, I quit the oil industry and much to my parents' and my bank manager's bewilderment, I went to art school, because I had always had this unspoken yearning to study art, although I didn't know if I would be any good at it. I had been engaging in creative work when I was still working as an engineer. In the Middle East and also when I was living in a hotel room in Trafalgar Square where my wife and I stayed for six months while we were waiting to buy a flat when I was posted back from the Middle East. We were in a very small, tight little hotel room but I was doing painting and graphics, as well as getting out early before work to do photography in the streets of London. I was doing all this for the love of it, because I needed to, initially with no thought of putting together a portfolio. But as I developed my ideas, I started thinking about applying to an art school, so I put all this work into a portfolio and took it around a few schools, and I was accepted to do a foundation course at Exeter College of Art.

I explored all kinds of areas such as graphics and sculpture and art and design. I was in my element. In my early thirties, I at last felt at home and was among people I could relate to. Most of the tutors were about the same age as me. During that year, my interest tended towards design. I think this was what interested me most because of my more practical background in engineering. Then, purely by chance, I found a postgraduate course at the Royal College of Art, RCA, in Industrial Design Engineering. It was a Master of Arts in Design that was set up for engineering graduates and was jointly offered by the RCA and Imperial College of Science. I was accepted onto that course, and it was during those studies that I started to focus on environmental approaches to design.

My major project at the end of the two years was a low-power electric-storage cooker with micro hydro generators. I modelled it on the computer and built a full-sized visual model. And that is really what set my new direction.

From the RCA, I joined the University of Calgary in Canada as a lecturer and researcher. In Calgary, I further developed my interest in design for sustainability, and it has just been expanding and growing ever since.

My first book on this subject was called Sustainable by Design, and in putting it together, I created numerous conceptual designs that explored different approaches to the topic. Ever since, I've tried to continue that design practice element of my research. That was one of the reasons I left engineering. I decided to make the move to art and design because I wanted to learn through practice rather than just through theory and rational, systematic analysis. So, practice was something that I wanted to maintain throughout my research, and I found that this is actually surprisingly unusual in academia. This seems absurd to me because design is a practice-based discipline. If you want to find out anything about design you have to practise, you have to learn it through practice. If you don't learn it through practice, you will just be intellectualising it, and it is not an intellectual kind of discipline. Only

Fig. 1: Providing student feedback, University of the Aegean, Syros, Greece, 2017

Fig. 2: Delivering the keynote talk, Design Commit Conference, Portugal, 2024

"The very term design thinking is fallacious because design is not just thinking. Design is *thinking and doing*. It is fundamentally a *practice-based* discipline."

some of it is. Half of it is the thinking. But the notion of 'design thinking' is fallacious—design is always 'thinking-and-doing'. It is fundamentally a practice-based discipline. Of course, you have got to think, and you have got to work things out intellectually, but that is not enough. It only becomes design when it is thinking and doing, working together.

K S Thinking and doing, blending theory and practice, ultimately leads to producing something?

S W   Yes, but I would say a word of caution here. Before starting my academic

14

career at the University of Calgary, I had already been through art school, which I think was very important because I had been taught at a practice-based, studio-based art school. At Calgary, one group I taught about design was made up of mechanical engineering students and there was a considerable difference between how they thought and worked compared with art and design students.

If I set a design project to students with a background in art and design, they tended to develop a range of conceptual solutions, which might not be functionally effective, they might not be able to work, they might not even be functionally feasible, but they would often be very creative and imaginative, and they might be very beautiful. If I set that same project to a class of engineers, they would come up with solutions that were functional, prototypes that could actually work. But these solutions were not very imaginative, and they certainly were not beautiful. And what I found to be a very difficult challenge when I was teaching these mechanical engineering students was to encourage them to come up with a variety of potential solutions to a problem. They would arrive at a design solution, and I would say, "Well, why don't you think up some other possible ways you could do this, some other conceptual approaches for how you might solve this?" And very often they would look at me with a puzzled expression and say, "What's the point of that? This works. So, there's no point in looking at anything else, because this one will work well."

But an important aspect of teaching design is to encourage imaginative exploration of a variety of possibilities, and critically assess their pros and cons before settling on a particular way forward. If you come up with one way of doing something, then you try to find a different way of doing it and then another way and another, so you have all these different conceptual approaches for dealing with something, and then you can see which might be the most effective or the most beautiful or the easiest to use, or the most cost-effective. This way, you can assess from within a range of possibilities. You do not just go for the first, most rational, systematically analysed solution to get to something that will work as though that is it. But this tended to be the approach I encountered among the engineering students, which is very narrow, convergent thinking. One of the things we were taught at art school, and that was very important for me, was to think much more divergently to open up your mind, and not to go for the first possible, most obvious way of doing something. And I found the engineers' way of thinking, which had been mine, rather intransigent. They were not used to that divergent way of thinking.

In my own case, I remember very clearly when the penny dropped. It was on the foundation course at Exeter. Our tutor was an artist, and we had been given a particular project to explore sculpture. I forget what it was exactly, but it was something involving found materials. We were asked to make some sort of sculpture. So, I went to the nearby beach to look for materials, like driftwood and pebbles and different stuff. I brought all this back to the studio, and I made a sculpture from driftwood and stones and string. And then the tutor came round in the studio to talk to each student. When it was my turn, he said, "Well, tell me about this construction you've made.", and so I explained to him what I had been aiming for and what I was trying to achieve. And he said, "OK, that's really interesting, and you've made it." And then he walked away to the next student, and I called him back. And I said, "So, is it right?" And he looked at me as if I was off my head. He said, "What do you mean?" And the penny dropped that I was still thinking like an engineer. I was still an engineer, and I was looking for a right answer and a wrong answer. He said, "That's not the point, is it? There is no right or wrong." And this incident made me realise that I was in a wholly different place here. These people speak in a different language. They have different priorities, and that revelation opened things up for me.

Creativity is a very different way of learning, a very different way of opening up and developing ideas. And how do those two ways come together? Can they come together? I'm not sure, but I am sure the best way to try is to be open to divergent

Fig. 3: Keynote talk, 2013

approaches and a more holistic way of thinking. Even though the sciences and engineering are applied subjects, they are not necessarily working in those divergent thinking areas that are more conceptual, creative and imaginative. They are still generally very systematic, rationalised, and intellectual. So, it is not just a case of being applied, it is more than that. It is about being creative and using your imaginative potential. And it is about valuing things that currently tend not to be valued very much. In these other, more divergent approaches, there is a considerable amount of tacit knowledge, ways of knowing that are inexpressible in words. You have to feel it.

K S I was really impressed when you sent us this article that focused on the problem of spirituality in design that you talk about in your book Design and Spirituality. And I was wondering what people in the design community would say about it. Because, of course, it really crosses boundaries. It goes in many directions. But there was no discussion about your article in my design community. There was no discussion because designers do not like to read, and designers are often simply not interested in society, the environment, or sustainable business practices. They just want to be artists, and they think they are better designers than others. They just want to be famous and make a lot of money. And you as an engineer, how did you give that up, because I think you could have made good money in the desert. Why did you not play that game? Is there something in your youth, in your family? Did you perhaps grow up in a socialist tradition?

S W   For sure. Yes, for sure. I come from a very socialist tradition. I come from the coal and steel valleys of South Wales. It is where the Trade Union Movement started in Britain. It is where the National Health Service started. The former Member of Parliament of my hometown of Ebbw Vale, Aneurin Bevan, spearheaded the creation of the National Health Service in Britain.

My approach to design and design research is fundamentally egalitarian and actually a lot of my design work, my early design work, where I created chairs using old found planks and anything I could find, those designs were directly inspired by my time working in the steelworks in my youth. It was a nationalised industry, and it was very over-manned and all around the steelworks, there were many, many small cabins where the workers, the labourers and steel workers, would go to have tea. And in these cabins, they often made the furniture out of any old material they could find to put together. They used planks and pieces of foam and nails and so on. Chairs, tables, even beds, which tells you something about how over-manned it was. But even then, I noticed these spontaneous designs because I was always struck by how comfortable they were, and yet, there was no pretension about this kind of design. A design was just hacked together so it would work and be comfortable, and these chairs and beds were always very comfortable, and they worked well. So, I was thinking, well, "What was wrong with that? That is working." On the face of it, this might seem like the same approach I was criticising earlier where the mechanical engineering students were coming up with solutions that worked. But, in fact, this approach by largely uneducated labourers in the steelworks was rather different. These chairs and tables and beds were not the result of over-intellectualised, systematic thinking. They were the result of a wholly practice-based way of working that was purely intuitive and free from all other pretensions or considerations. These objects were not going to be exhibited or marketed or sold, and no one was concerned about them having to be beautiful. They just had to be comfortable, and they were made from whatever materials could be found. So, this is actually a very sustainable design because it is using rather than creating waste. And there is a humility to it. And so, if you looked at them from a certain point of view, you could say that these objects possessed a certain kind of beauty. They were not over-intellectualised, but neither were they sullied by designer affectations.

I was looking at these designs even then, even in my teens, and thinking, "That

DESIGNERS CAN SHOW WHAT POSITIVE CHANGE LOOKS LIKE

Fig. 4:
Low Chair

Fig. 5:
Codex Morte

Fig. 6:
Hermit Radio

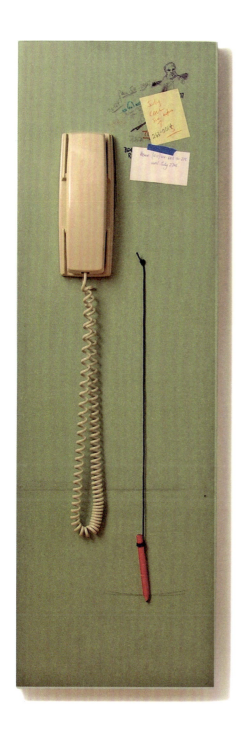

Fig. 7:
Re-Call

Fig. 8:
Lather Lamp

is really interesting. This can be so comfortable, and yet there is no awareness of design here. These guys have put this together so that it works well. You can see the same ways of working in street furniture made by people who just knock things together on the side of the street, just so that the thing, whatever it is, works. I find it fascinating that we can design in such ways. There is a naivety but there is also a kind of purity to that.

Design changes as soon as you say, "I am a designer." It puts a different kind of spin on things. The work becomes knowingly designed. And so, I wanted to see if that could actually be stripped out. Of course, it may not be possible. To consciously design unconsciously? In the new book that I am putting together, I talk about this. I have photographs of two chairs I created some years ago, just from bits of wood. I used anything I had to hand, and I was deliberately trying to extract any hint of me from it. I just wanted it to be functional. I did not want it to be about me. I did not want it to be about looking at it and asking myself, "Is it beautiful?" I just wanted to work intuitively, and I wanted it to work as a functioning chair. And so I made a chair. And I looked at it and I sealed the surface of the wood with a wash of watered-down scrap paint I happened to have nearby, which was an awful pink colour. But it was at hand and so it was good enough. That was the premise of the approach I was taking.

I looked at the final chair and the structure was working well, it was solid, it was stable, it was simple, and it was easy to put together. But then I decided that I wasn't very happy with the way it looked. So, then I created another one. I changed the proportions a little, making the seat a little larger, and I visually separated the seat and the back, those parts where the human body touches, by using a different colour paint from the rest. This second chair was basically the same as the first one, but it had more pleasing proportions, and it had a more pleasing appearance because of the two different colours. And then I asked myself, "Is that OK, is that acceptable?" The original chair was done without any thought of appearance. And the later one is essentially the same chair, and yet it is not. It is different. It has got something else. And what is that something else? And is it good? Yes, maybe it looks a little better, but is that a good transition? Is that what the transition is about? And is this what it should be about? In thinking about these things, I was asking myself, "Is it too much? Is it going too far? Is it becoming too self-aware compared with the first chair, which is not?"

These are the kinds of issues that interest me. What does the transition to design actually mean? I'm not sure I have any firm answers, but it's those types of questions that I've always asked myself, which I've struggled with. These are the issues I think about and investigate. Then, when you think about my background, design and spirituality, all these things are deeply related to what I've just been talking about.

Scientists and engineers really bought into and accepted modernity. And they tend to be gung-ho about innovation and the new. But when you look at the history of the world, just to put all this innovation into another context, climate change and environmental destruction started in earnest around 1750. That was the start of the Industrial Revolution. Since then, it has just been on an exponential upward curve of destruction and emissions. Primarily, this is due to modernity, which is the development of industrial society. Also, when you look at the history of the human population, it was very, very slowly rising over 10,000 years or more. A very slow, shallow rise. We reached about 1750 and from that point on, the human population of the earth started to rise exponentially and so the overpopulation of the world, the destruction of natural environments, biodiversity decline, species decline, and global emissions all started in earnest with modernity.

Modernity has brought us wonderful medical developments, more comfortable lives, hot water in the home, sanitation, and convenience. We can drive around in our comfortable cars, and we live in well-heated homes.

> "It is all great for some of us, but we are a very *small proportion* of the population of the world. To provide us with these comforts, the rest of the world is being *exploited* and *polluted*."

This means our own world is being exploited and polluted. And all this goes against spiritual teachings in every culture, and I mean in every culture.

When I was growing up, I went to church every week. I listened to the Gospels, I listened to the sermon, as many people of my generation did in those days. In my teens, I rejected it all. I thought this was a lot of rubbish, I could not believe it. But it has never left me and even in my mid-twenties when I was studying mining engineering, I would always find myself in the religious section of the second-hand bookshop near the university, looking around and buying and reading because it fascinated me. Even though, all the time,

I was thinking that I did not accept it, it was a load of bunk. But part of me was also telling me that it has been around for 2,000 years and a great number of very intelligent people still talk about it in a very thoughtful, meaningful way, so perhaps it is me. Perhaps I am missing something.

To cut a long story short, it has stayed with me all the way through. I have continued to read Christian texts as well as Daoist, Hindu, Buddhist and Islamic texts, to try to understand. The conclusion I have come to is that, essentially, they are all the same in terms of their essential messages, even if these messages are dressed in different clothes. In the case of Jesus and the Buddha, there is different window dressing if you like. They have different ways of expressing essentially the same thing. And when you look at the fundamental messages of Christianity or any of the other great religions, they are on the opposite side of the value spectrum from modernity. Modernity is about innovation, it's about constant change, it's about personal ambition and social status, and in consumer-capitalist economies, it has become about profligacy, hedonism, the constant churn of change, never having enough and always wanting more. On the opposite side of the value spectrum, there is an emphasis on ecology and looking after the natural world, benevolence and looking after other people, community, respecting traditions, and seeing the benefits of stability and conservation. All these things resonate strongly with spiritual teachings, which are essentially about goodness and virtue. But, in many ways, modernity has come to represent the very opposite. So, when you think about spiritual teachings and their relationship to the natural world and to our neighbours, our immediate neighbours and the people in our own community, as well as people in the world in general, they are all

"There are many benefits of *modernity*, but the cost is far too high. And there are many things to learn from *spiritual traditions*, which in modernity, we have just *dismissed as being irrelevant*."

on the opposite side of the spectrum from those values being prioritised by modern, consumption-based societies. That is where spirituality is and where modernity is not. Climate change and the overpopulation of the Earth has occurred during modernity, and that is due to modernity's values and priorities. Spiritual traditions have lasted 2,000 years, or in some cases much longer. They represent very different values and priorities, which are very much in line with contemporary thinking in the sphere of sustainability.

Up to the beginning of modernity, people knew about and paid attention to traditional spiritual teachings much more than they do now, and the world was being sustained. Human populations were being maintained at sustainable levels. Yes, there were diseases which we couldn't cure. Yes, there was considerable infant mortality. There were not the technologies and the conveniences and the comforts that we have today. But we were not putting the whole world or the whole human population in jeopardy. So how do you get this balance right? What is the right relationship? This interests me. It isn't a case of one

side or the other. And we do not need to go back to that time. There are many benefits of modernity, but the cost is far too high. And there are many things to learn from spiritual traditions, which in modernity, we have just dismissed as being irrelevant. Some of the so-called new atheists such as Richard Dawkins and Anthony Grayling and others talk about religion in such disparaging terms. But they tend to speak about it from the point of view of a literalist interpretation and an ignorance about what these texts are really saying. What I have found through my readings of these spiritual texts is that they are not easy. And the most difficult ones, in my view, are the Christian texts because they are written in such a way that it is all too easy to read them at a literal level. But when you do this, they immediately become implausible. A rational thinking person cannot accept many of these things, such as a man walking on water and changing water into wine. If you read them on a literal level, of course you can't believe them. But you have to look behind the literal meaning to find out what they are really getting at. You can't find this if you stay at the literal level. They

Fig. 9: After delivering the keynote talk at the China Summit, Coventry, 2022

seem like so much nonsense. However, they need to be contemplated, and you have to say to yourself, "If it seems like nonsense in the way I'm reading it, then what is it really about? If it's still being read after 2,000 years, it must mean something that I am missing." I find this fascinating.

K S Yes, me too. Maybe because we were all children of modernity, we had this too mechanical view of the world. And there was no place for spirituality.

S W   I think so, yes.

K S You know a lot about the problematic situations in the world, but you work in your community for the better. What keeps you optimistic?

S W   Maybe I'm just deluded, but you know, when Pandora opened the box, the only thing that was left inside was hope. If you don't have hope, you don't have anything.

I think we have the ability to change. What gives me hope, in a perverse kind of way, is that when we changed from the mediaeval mindset, with God at the top and then the king, the knights and the serfs, to modernity, which was about progress and looking to the future, that change probably took about 300 to 400 years. This shows us that we can change. During those centuries, we changed our entire worldview.

If we changed so fundamentally once, we have the potential to change again. I think, this time, we need to change more rapidly, and in some ways, it is much more difficult because with global communications, there are very powerful persuaders, and many vested interests in staying the same. But we do have to change and change quickly. We do not have 300 to 400 years. But it's more difficult because there is such a machine in place now in marketing and politics. Everything is in place to keep the train going in the same direction. And there is a great deal of investment going into confusing the debate. There is investment from the oil industry to confuse the debate around climate change, to put doubt in people's minds in the same way that, for years, the tobacco industry deliberately confused the debate about smoking and its links to cancer. Today, we know what the dangers are, and they are becoming more and more acute. The need for change is going to become more and more urgent. The mass migration that we are seeing these days is partly due to climate change and lack of opportunity. But also, there are the people in other countries living in poverty, whose resources have been exploited for years through colonialism, and later

Fig. 10

through globalised capitalism, which have enabled us to become relatively rich and comfortable. With global communications via the Internet, those people can now see what they are missing and quite naturally, they are asking themselves why those people over there have all the good stuff. They would like some of that too, of course they would, and they should never have been exploited in the first place. In the past, it was easier to hoodwink people. So, I think we are going through a very significant change. Global communications are still a very recent phenomenon.

It is difficult to remain optimistic when you see the state of the natural environment and the current state of play, and when you realise that certain people are trying to keep things the same. Also, the scale of the impacts that are coming to meet us, I think it's very significant. But in order to effect positive change, whatever area we are in, whether we are an accountant or a civil engineer, or a design academic, we have to do what we can within our own sphere of influence to create that change. And in that regard, I think designers and design researchers are in a uniquely important position. That is not to say that designers are at the centre of the world, but what designers can do is what other disciplines are less able to do, and that is to visualise and show alternative, potentially better, futures. Designers can help reduce nervousness around change by showing what positive change can actually look like. Visualising it and envisioning different ways of being, different ways of behaving, different ways of living. Showing that this could be better than what we have now. Designers can paint that picture more effectively than most other disciplines. It is a task that is deeply meaningful and tremendously worthwhile.

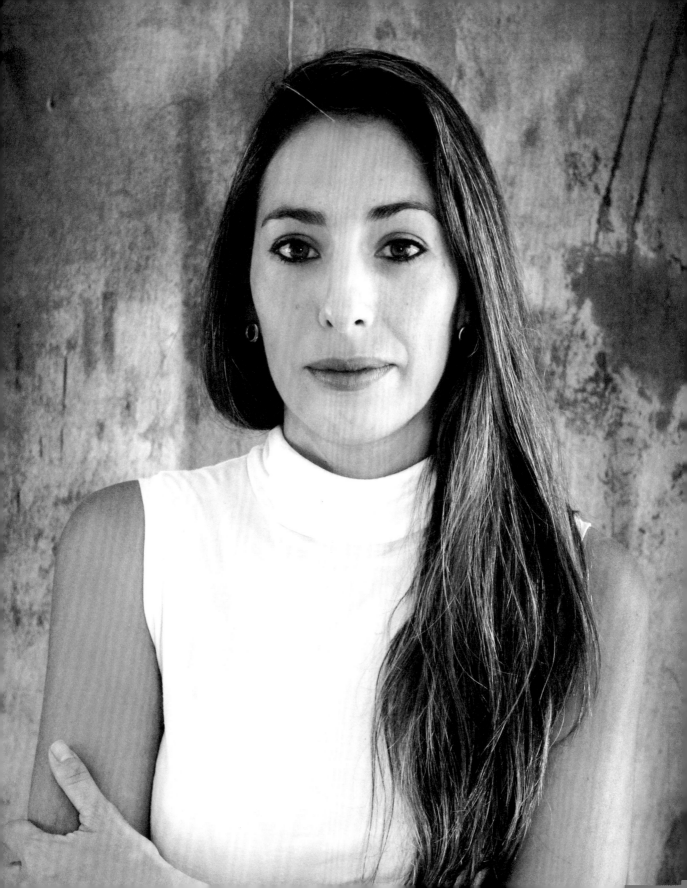

Words by　　　　　Lilián González-González

Creating A
Design Manual

LILIÁN GONZÁLEZ-GONZÁLEZ is an industrial designer and Academic Coordinator at Anáhuac University of Mexico. She currently serves as a board advisor for the World Design Organization, where she was previously a board member from 2022 to 2023. Additionally, she is on the editorial board of the magazine worldesign by Domus and is a member on the board of advisors and jury for the Don Norman Design Award. Lilián holds a PhD in Critical Theory, focusing on social design experience for the common good, a Certificate in Critical Theory on Disability and Inclusion. She obtained her Master's degree in Contemporary Art and a Specialty Certificate in Art in Florence, Italy. With a diverse professional background, Lilián has worked as both a designer in the industry and a professor at various universities across Mexico. She is actively engaged as a director, organizer, speaker, and curator for numerous international awards, conferences, talks, symposiums, and exhibitions on art and design worldwide.

CREATING A DESIGN MANUAL

(L)(G) For over eight years, I have been developing a design manual to help students and professionals address complex social challenges and conflicts within marginalized contexts, with the goal of fostering hope.

The design manual focuses on promoting reflection on objects and the interaction with them, from a perspective enriched by theory and critical imagination. It applies these insights to social design, specifically the creation of experiences for the common good. From this approach arises an initial observation of how relationships with objects have been evolving, adapting to a life that demands new attributes and characteristics from them, as well as the capacity to generate more complex interactions, as occurs with more sophisticated ones.

This manual includes reflections from various fields of knowledge, such as critical theory, philosophy, art, literature, linguistics, and other areas of the humanities and social sciences. These perspectives can offer valuable insights to the design discipline, enabling the creation of unique and meaningful objects with transformative, symbolic, disruptive, and instituting powers. The aim is to establish significant foundations for the creation of objects that promote dialectical and emancipatory processes, rather than those that enslave, control, or alienate people. Today, it is imperative to denounce, reverse, generate and regenerate new and creative design logics that encourage significant changes among people.

The result of the research I conducted during my doctoral study was a journey of experimentation, improvisation, imagination, and the desire to develop a methodological guide to assist teachers and design students in the creation of unique objects with the potential to make significant changes socially and individually.

At the outset of the research project, I critically questioned the status quo of design methodologies and tools, tracing their transformations throughout history in relation to critical theory and art. I relied on texts that kept the research project alive and that served as a guide to conclude the research. The fundamental ideas that shaped my approach include Jean Baudrillard's notion of singularity, Friedrich Nietzsche's text On Truth and Lies as a means of exploring metaphor. This exploration then led me to delve into Walter Benjamin's writings on the culture industry and the works of Theodor W. Adorno.

These reflections stirred questions in me about how to promote teaching including critical theory so that designers can create objects for current and future problems, rather than continually resorting to traditional forms of design. Aspiring that the result would be the creation of design objects that raise insightful questions and reflections beyond the obvious and superficial. Objects that not only respond to desire, but also to fear, pain, hurt, frustration, and hopelessness. How can we, as designers, respond to these human questions—decentering design from the focus of desire and moving it toward the notion of affect?

It is precisely this context in which my doctoral research project was born. Returning to the notion of the common good as understood from the concepts of Aristotle, Saint Thomas Aquinas, and Jacques Maritain. From Maritain's perspective, individuality includes aspects such as matter, body, health, hygiene, vitality, personality, spirituality, values, principles, ethics, and morality—dimensions that I integrated into the project's methodological and analytical framework

Fig. 1: Altar of the Death/Mexican's Ritual
Collaboration project, art and design concept by Lilián González-González

as key reflections throughout the process, all closely connected to community.

This last point highlights how personal satisfaction is achieved from encounters with others in the community, in this case, such interactions are facilitated through the design of experiences, emotional design, and behavioral design, which are integral to the ideation stages leading to the project's final solutions. For Maritain, individuality and community are not dichotomously separated elements, but rather they can be harmonized. Therefore, the common good is not the end, but the means to ultimate fulfillment. We cannot separate the satisfaction of individual desire from that of the community; instead, we should concentrate efforts on creating design solutions that address both individual and communal needs, as a unified whole.

From this, I also reviewed the concepts of symbolic interactivity, experience design, and emotional design. I was therefore analyzing how people's relationship with objects and the world around them can affect and, thereby, enhance significant changes in individuals and communities. In particular, symbolic interaction dynamically generates new behaviors and sensitivities at both the individual and collective level (PONS DIEZ 2010).

As I investigated these concepts and how all this influenced objects and people, I gradually applied them in my undergraduate Industrial Design class at Anáhuac University in Mexico City. I tried applying them with all types of themes and saw that the results generated were objects with greater uniqueness, complexity, and critical reflection. Our first topic was the 2017 earthquake in Mexico City, a deeply impactful event for all of us. The result was an installation that moved closer to the realm of art, but at least managed to generate metaphorical bridges, testimonial, and emptying from the design.

Of course, I made many mistakes along the way that helped me continue improving the methodological instrument. Academic timelines are very short, so balancing between the rush, student impatience, and my experimentation processes presented challenges sometimes. We tackled projects in diverse settings, such as impoverished areas and rehabilitation centers for children with cerebral palsy. Without extensive experience in these issues, but with the help of experts, we were able to achieve results. Designing with an understanding of the complexity of these issues, driven by intuition and motivation to create meaningful differentiated results for the common good, helped us reach the objective.

In the design discipline, we are full of methodologies that turn out to be quick guides with very useful tools. However, my fear was always to generate a methodology that could accelerate a type of design thinking that was not common, and that is now approached from critical theory, philosophy, and art.

Over the course of eight years, experimenting semester after semester, I incorporated critical theoretical ingredients, removing, improvising, and experimenting along the way. This process also

created uncertainty among the students, so I began to develop the methodological guide for design.

Furthermore, I have to mention that when I arrived at the design academy, where I developed all these projects, concepts for social and sustainable issues, design toward the common good, and experience design were not well understood, and methodologies related to social issues were not applied. They were rather projects oriented towards the design of collections, furniture, and object art. As a result, the direction and strategy of the Industrial Design School changed as I began to apply social issues alongside the design tools that helped to develop these projects.

Fig. 2: Installation created by Anáhuac University industrial design students at Design Week Mexico 2017 in Lincoln Park, Mexico City-titled Huiznahuac, Nahuatl for ferocactus biznaga-commemorating the victims of the earthquake on September 19 2017.

How can we address the uniqueness, the specific problems and find solutions for communities, or marginal situations?

First, the focus should be on connecting the designers with the communities or individuals facing specific challenges or problems, using innovative solutions that have not been proposed by the existing designs. This approach involves designing with people, employing co-design tools, and integrating critical theory as the starting point for project analysis. Accompanied by a methodology that continually calls into question the probability and confronts challenges to transform them into singular, instituting objects that offer hope to communities and serve as an engine to continue building a better future.

Carrying out field visits is essential for observation, and interviews contribute significantly to the designer's awareness. This stage is undoubtedly contemplated in design methodologies and favors the designer's intuition to reach viable solutions for people. However, I observed that the research lacked further reflection on critical theory. Therefore, I assumed the role of facilitator of critical thinking.

From the first stages of the research, I guided the students toward reading theoretical and critical reflections, along with relevant conferences, podcasts, and documentaries on the problems being studied, to deepen their critical thinking. This methodology allowed the designer to develop a reflective understanding, favoring critical thinking from the beginning of the investigation, altering their perception of reality. Through this approach, the designer can imagine possibilities based on the current situation, visualize the impossible, and conceive hope for people through design—transforming what initially seems unattainable into something possible, while respecting the uniqueness of each project.

The teaching manual prepared within the framework of this doctoral research integrates moments of reflection, analysis, and imagination across its various steps and areas of knowledge, enriching the design processes. It guides designers throughout the entire research journey and has significantly impacted the design outcomes at the university where it has been implemented. Furthermore, it cultivates social awareness and deepens the students' understanding of their own context, enabling them to envision solutions that contribute to the common good.

CREATING A DESIGN MANUAL

Design From Critical Theory
For The Common Good

 Critical theory

 Design steps

 Research

32

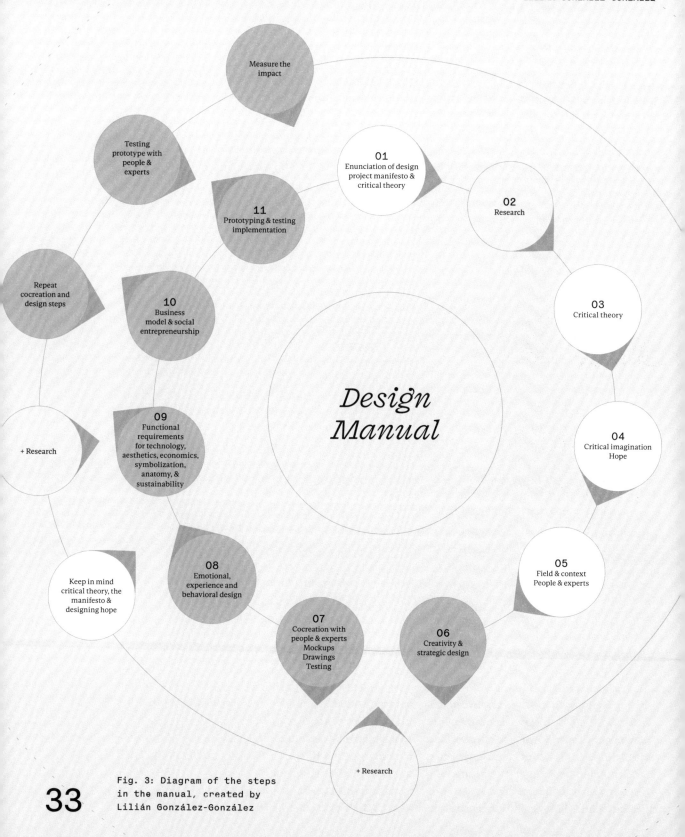

Fig. 3: Diagram of the steps in the manual, created by Lilián González-González

CREATING A DESIGN MANUAL

DESIGN FOR HOPE

PRESENT

Faith   Prolongation of suffering

Hope   Utopia   Illusion

STATES OF PAIN, VIOLENCE, MARGINALIZATION, EXCLUSION...

Acceptance   Reconciliation

Human suffering   Chaos

FUTURE

DESIGN FROM PEACE

The following arguments are antagonistic to each other, since they represent completely opposite positions on the subject. Hope as an active and collective energy that mobilizes people towards the creation of a better world. Hope, in his vision, has a transformative dimension (BLOCH 2007). Suffering and chaos are an intrinsic part of life, and tragedy allows human beings to accept and reconcile themselves with that suffering rather than fleeing from it through illusions such as hope (NIETZSCHE 2007).

Fig. 4: Design From Peace & Design For Hope, Lilián González-González

34

"Critical theory has been the central guiding thread of this work, with its *philosophical, sociological,* and *political* approach focused on the *transformation of society*. Originating from the Frankfurt School in the twentieth century, it critiques *power structures, dominant ideologies,* and *social injustices*."

In Mexico, 60 percent of university students attend public universities, the rest go to private institutions. Some private universities are Catholic and, as such, incorporate a social mission and the common good into their educational model. This context made it especially relevant to introduce tools that would help design students develop social projects and, more importantly, transform knowledge into conscious action based on their context and reality. This is achieved through the inclusion of critical theory, which is embedded in the design manual throughout the design steps.

But what is critical theory, and why is it so important in the design process—and in any discipline? As previously mentioned, this research has been built on the support of critical theory, alongside current design methodologies and tools, with the goal of strengthening the results oriented towards design of experiences for the common good.

Critical theory has been the central guiding thread of this work, with its philosophical, sociological, and political approach focused on the transformation of society. Originating from the Frankfurt School in the twentieth century, it critiques power structures, dominant ideologies, and social injustices. Therefore, in addition to reflecting on social situations, the objective is to provoke significant change that promotes greater social justice, processes of emancipation and, therefore, well-being—principles aligned with the common good that this manual aims to support. As Max Horkheimer states, "Critical theory is not only an instrument to interpret the world; it is also a means to change it. The ultimate goal is the emancipation of human beings from conditions of oppression and exploitation" (HORKHEIMER 2002).

Based on this idea, one of the premises throughout the research is that design can be a transformative force, impacting human development, living conditions, and social and cultural ties to overcome the realities of oppression, exploitation, and violence in which we live. Peace coexists with differences and their resulting conflicts, which is an inevitable part of the human experience. While conflict can be both destructive and transformative, it ultimately drives change, growth, and creative problem-solving. The key is to learn how to manage conflict constructively through dialogue, empathy, and mutual understanding.

What should we aim to design? Perhaps objects with the power to inspire hope for a better future—fulfilling basic human and planetary needs, making education accessible, plus achieving personal contentment and recognition. As Escobar (2018, p. 13) suggests, "We are creating ways of being."

At this time, I believe the next step of change should be to broaden the application of the design manual, expanding its use beyond educational settings to include professional and collaborative practices in social design. While fostering a pedagogy that integrates critical theory and codesign tools, it is equally important to extend these practices, involving designers and communities who are directly engaged with social issues, particularly in marginalized and vulnerable situations. Above all, this manual should serve as a resource for the application of various disciplines in design to promote significant changes in the lives of people and the earth.

Furthermore, strengthening the relationship between designers and communities is vital to ensure that the design process remains dialogical and collaborative. This not only helps designers create meaningful and unique objects, but also enables solutions to emerge from the specific needs and hopes of the communities themselves. Real transformation occurs when design becomes a platform for social change, challenging oppressive structures and building a more equitable and emancipated society.

Another essential aspect of this next step is to systematically measure the transformative impact of these projects. Assessing how this methodology contributes to meaningful change at both individual and community levels is crucial. Tracking outcomes will provide insights into the effectiveness of the design process in promoting hope, well-being, and social justice, while also offering opportunities to refine the approach and amplify its impact.

In closing, the design manual represents a significant advancement in addressing complex social issues, particularly within marginalized contexts. Extending its principles beyond the academic environment, encouraging closer collaboration between designers, other disciplines, and communities will ensure the design process responds to real, tangible needs. Systematically measuring the transformative effects of these projects will also allow ongoing refinement of the methodology and enhance its impact. By grounding design in critical theory and community engagement, we can contribute to creating objects that not only address immediate challenges but also inspire hope and drive positive, lasting change in society.

REFERENCES

BLOCH 2007 = Bloch, Ernst (2007) El principio esperanza (Vols. 1–3, Ed. Trotta). Frankfurt: Suhrkamp Verlag (Original work published 1959)
HORKHEIMER 2002 = Horkheimer, Max (2002) Traditional and critical theory. In: Critical theory: Selected essays (188-243). New York: CONTINUUM (Original work published 1937)

NIETZSCHE 2007 = Nietzsche, Friedrich (2007) El nacimiento de la tragedia (A. Sánchez Pascual, Trad.). Alianza Editorial (Original work published 1872)
PONS DIEZ 2010 = Pons Diez, Javier (2010) La aportación a la psicología social del interaccionismo simbólico: una revisión histórica. Dialnet, 9, 23-42.

FURTHER READING

Adorno, Theodor W. / Horkheimer, Max (1944) La industria cultural: Ilustración como engaño de masas. En Dialectic of Enlightenment. New York: Continuum
Baudrillard, Jean (2007) Los objetos singulares: arquitectura y filosofía. Buenos Aires: Fondo de Cultura Económica
Escobar, Arturo (2018) Design for the pluriverse: Radical interdependence, autonomy, and the making of worlds. Duke University Press

González, Lilián (2022). Blog publication. In: https://designforsociety.org/2022/04/09/altar-of-the-death-mexicans-ritual/[10/12/2024]
Nietzsche, Friedrich (1996) Sobre verdad y mentira en sentido extramoral, Hans Vaihinger. En La voluntad de ilusión en Nietzsche (L. M. Orduña, Trad.). Madrid: Tecnos

Words by   Gunnar Rundgren

Swimming In A River
Of Change

GUNNAR RUNDGREN is a farmer, consultant, critical thinker, and author based in Sunnansjö, Sweden. He became engaged in environmental issues in his teenage years. Through a confluence of subjective choices, coincidences, and external impulses, he began organic farming, established various organizations, and worked as an international consultant. Nowadays, Rundgren focuses on writing and food production. His main interest is exploring the expansion of the role of commons and decentralizing the management of society and nature at the expense of both central governments and the markets.

G R I think my first awakening about environmental issues was when my mother explained the link between detergents and the algal bloom in the lake at my grandparents' place where I spent my summers up to the age of eleven. At a young age, I was already concerned with how cars polluted the environment and how many people were being killed or maimed. At the age of 13, my best friend and I joined a bicycle activist group in our hometown Uppsala. The group organized political demonstrations and collected signatures for petitions against parking garages and new roads. We quickly became core activists, working with much older individuals, which when you are 13 means that they were only twenty.

Through the protests against the war in Vietnam, my interests in general politics grew with an anarchist inclination. Meanwhile, my environmental concern pursued with an increased focus on nuclear power. Protests against atomic energy were intense and led to a moratorium on new nuclear power plants in 1980. Although the decision also decreed that the existing reactors should be closed down, it never came to fruition, and many of them are still running today, over four decades later.

At the age of 18, I had come to the conclusion that it was not enough just to protest. There was an urgent need to develop practical solutions for both the environmental and social crises, ideally addressing both simultaneously. I connected with like-minded people, and together we began to plan for the establishment of an agrarian commune. Our focus being social development and environmentally friendly technologies with a strong emphasis on self-sufficiency. We were motivated by our awareness of the significant corrupting forces within the dominant society.

After some preparation, in February 1977, five of us moved into the Torfolk farm in the middle of Värmland, Sweden. The first years were dedicated to learning all the necessary skills for a relatively self-sufficient lifestyle. This included not only growing crops and tending to animals but also things like tanning moose hide, making cheese and butter, logging, knitting, and weaving. To help with forestry and some agricultural tasks, we used a horse. Among us, one member had an education in agriculture, another had some skills in welding, and a third was adept in weaving. I drew inspiration and knowledge from my mother, who taught farming and home economics—a subject that covers the care of livestock and crops, as well as their processing into food. My father was almost a caricature of a professor, who could neither handle a hammer nor fry an egg.

My partner at the time, Kari, took a job in the city to provide the income necessary to pay off the mortgage and cover our investments. We lived on a tight budget. Initially, we had plans to expand the commune and welcomed visitors with open arms. Back then, many young people were searching for alternatives as the hippie and back-to-the-land movements were very popular. Naturally, we had many visitors. Some stayed a week, while others remained for several months at a time. Although several of the founders left, they were quickly replaced by new members. After a few years, we grew weary of the constant turnover, and implemented stricter guidelines for admitting new members, though we never made it onerous to join. For many years in the beginning, we consisted of five members. After that, for almost 20 years, we had been operating the farm as a group of four, two couples to be exact. In some regards, we were highly communitarian, sharing our income equally. Each of us used the communal funds responsibly, and since we

Fig. 1: Distilling peppermint oil at Torfolk

had so little, this rarely posed a problem. When the children were old enough, they received pocket money. From my experience, there are more challenges when there is a lot of money, and people might want to go on vacation, buy luxury items or attend rock concerts. Additionally, we had no leader and seldom held formal meetings. Decisions were made at the dinner table, there was no written plan outlining our goals or methods of achieving them. At a relatively late stage, we attempted to implement more strategic planning. In regard to our approach to dealing with emotions, we rarely discussed our feelings and personal relationships. We were more traditional in this aspect.

Over time, our orientation changed, and we abandoned radical self-sufficiency and embarked on activities to generate income. We started with goat farming, cheese making, and growing vegetables. This shift was not the result of any formal decision, but rather a gradual evolution. One of the main reasons, as I recall, was the cognizance that by distancing ourselves too much from society, we also lost many opportunities for interaction and exchange. Just being a freak example would not change much. In 1980, my partner and I had our first child, and we realized that when you have children, you also need to consider that your choices impact them as well. And as they grow, peer pressure intensifies the desire to have similar things, do similar activities, and even believe in similar ideas. For example, if your child watches television at a friend's home you will likely want to buy one yourself. We also began to yearn for a bit more comfort and convenience, such as washing machines and chainsaws.

In addition, we were probably influenced by the change of the tides in the eighties, with more focus on self-fulfillment and ideas that you could actually change the system from within. Although we did not fully embrace the emerging neoliberalism, as with any other prevailing societal trend, it was hard not to be influenced by it. We believed that, with enough ingenuity, it would be possible to earn a living while still maintaining things with a small-scale thoughtful approach. So, we started the project with the utilization of modest, smart technologies for vegetable production and cheese making in order to be competitive.

From the onset, we operated organically, even if we followed no special organic method or had any kind of certification. Prior to the early nineties, when we officially started using the term "ekologisk" in Sweden, organic produce was either labeled as poison-free or biodynamic farming. However, this was more of a generic term that was not linked to a specific method. When we tried to market our growing vegetable production to the regional supermarkets, many of them got back to us and were interested in our products, especially the consumer cooperative Konsum, now Coop. They had decisions made by their membership assembly that they should start to sell organic products. In order to be an attractive supplier, we needed to stock up and offer a wider range of vegetables. In 1983, we rallied together a handful of organic growers and created the marketing cooperative Samodlarna for the sale of organic vegetables to supermarkets. To my knowledge, the first of its kind in Europe. The name we chose roughly translates to companion croppers, alluding to both the fact that we cooperate and that we often practiced companion planting. We established some simple rules to be followed by the members. We got the regional advisory service to allocate a person to verify that our members followed the rules. It was a rudimentary certification system. Our farm managed the marketing and administration of the organization.

The cooperative was successful and got a lot of attention. Our example spread and in winter 1984, we gathered like-minded people from other parts of Sweden for a few meetings where we discussed how to progress organic agriculture. At this time, the early organic pioneers, mostly farming biodynamically, had been joined by a group of more politically interested and environmentally motivated back-to-the-landers like us. The meetings resulted in a three-pronged institutional strategy for the organic movement with a National Marketing Association to further develop the organic market, an Ecological Farmers Association to pursue political acceptance and support of the label in addition to providing education about it and at last, the formation of the certification body KRAV in 1985. I became the first executive director of the organization and commuted seven hours by bus and train on a weekly basis between the farm and the KRAV office in Uppsala.

KRAV was founded by three organic associations, but already at the outset, the idea was to engage member organizations representing the whole food chain as well as environmental and animal welfare groups. The reasons for this were to augment the credibility of the organization and the certification as an impartial service as well as to ensure the support from the members

> "We wanted to formulate *organic standards* by inspecting and verifying that affiliated farmers and food producers followed the standards. In addition, we made it our goal *to educate* the public and promote organic products."

for the KRAV mark and organic products. We wanted to formulate organic standards by inspecting and verifying that affiliated farmers and food producers followed the standards. In addition, we made it our goal to educate the public and promote organic products.

In the process of establishing KRAV we also looked outside of Sweden to see how people had organized organic certification in other places. Established organizations, such as Nature et Progrès in France, which two of us visited in 1988, Soil Association in the UK, and California Certified Organic Farmers were a few that we drew inspiration from. We also realized that we shared common needs for the verification, audit, and certification of organic standards. This led me to the International Federation of Organic Agriculture Movements, IFOAM, founded in 1972. There, I got involved in the development of the Global Organic Guarantee System with the ambition to safeguard the integrity of organic products (IFOAM 2024). In 1993, I became the chairperson of the IFOAM accreditation program, later known as International Organic Accreditation Services, with the purpose of ensuring the quality of organic certification worldwide.

In a parallel development, the EU adopted a regulation for the marketing of organic products in 1992. The United States was also in the process of doing so. Most of the organic sector supported this development for three reasons: the general recognition of the relevance of organic agriculture which is implicit in a regulation; the increased possibility of getting government support for organic production and market development; and the lack of trust among actors in the organic sector, both nationally and internationally. It is often claimed that the regulations were developed to protect the consumers, but it is worth noting that there were hardly any consumer organizations demanding the regulation. The initiative to regulate was brought up by the producers themselves. They wanted to ensure a level playing field in the market, especially in France and Germany, where the sector was extremely fragmented. This last point was concerned with the fact that in most countries, there were many competing organic associations and certification bodies which often slandered each other, leading to suspicion and mistrust within the public. Our experiences in Sweden with a unifying independent certification scheme, which had a high level of public trust, made me opposed to any regulation as I feared that the definition of organic would be overtaken by the governments, which eventually happened.

I failed, however, to convince the majority of the organic sector that government regulations were a bad thing.

As a result of the success of KRAV and my involvement with IFOAM, I received a lot of requests to help with the establishment of national certification bodies and organic development in other countries. In 1995, I established the Grolink consultancy. From then on, it grew rapidly and at its height, around 2006, had a dozen associates, a turnover of approximately 3.5 million US dollars and operated in most continents.

Even though some of the core business was to help in the establishment of organic certification bodies, I gradually lost interest in certification as it had passed its pioneering era and been overtaken by regulations. Within the organic sector, I often found myself in opposition to those who demanded stricter and more detailed standards and certification rules. The rigidity of the system stifled innovation, experimentation and local adaptation. All of these are essential aspects of evolutionary change. In addition, it transferred most of the ownership of the organic project to governments and those with a full-time job to control the system, so-called organocrats. The rules also included provisions that prohibited certification bodies from assisting producers in terms of compliance and from participating in the promotion of organic products. Certification was, therefore, gradually taken over by professional multinational companies. Thus, a lot more money was spent on resources demonstrating that the label was reliable and trustworthy rather than on helping farmers or developing the market.

Perhaps this was inevitable, but I was more interested in things that would lead to development instead of trying to limit and restrict the sector. Gradually, I shifted my focus, both as a consultant and

Fig. 2: In discussion with a farmer and a farm advisor from Kasisi Agricultural Training Center in Zambia

Fig. 3: Putting up a sign post for vegatable sales, Sunnansjö farm, Sweden

as an organic activist, towards marketing, policy development and alike. From 2002 to 2008, Grolink managed a very successful project, EPOPA, for organic exports from Africa. It granted more than 100,000 smallholder farmers access to organic markets (RUNDGREN 2008). In addition, Grolink managed an international training program for the organic agriculture sector in developing countries that trained existing or presumptive sector leaders.

I was elected Vice President of IFOAM in 1998 and I was then President from 2000 to 2005. During my term, we initiated many policy processes and tried to position organic farming within the context of the Millennium Development Goals, the precursor to the Sustainable Development Goals. We also promoted participatory and group certification as alternatives to commercial ones. As the organic sector had been dominated by certifications, standards and market development, IFOAM also initiated a process to define and highlight the wider agenda embedded in organic agriculture. One of the accomplishments that I am particularly proud of was the development of the Principles of Organic Agriculture (see box). They represent somewhat of a retreat towards the roots of the organic movement, emphasizing that the term organic is much more than a market-oriented production method.

 THE PRINCIPLES OF ORGANIC AGRICULTURE

Principle of Health: Organic agriculture should sustain and enhance the health of soil, plant, animal, human and planet as one and indivisible.

Principle of Ecology: Organic agriculture should be based on living ecological systems and cycles, work with them, emulate them and help sustain them.

Principle of Fairness: Organic agriculture should build on relationships that ensure fairness with regard to the common environment and life opportunities.

Principle of Care: Organic agriculture should be managed in a precautionary and responsible manner to protect the health and well-being of current and future generations and the environment.

IFOAM 2023

The years as an international consultant and IFOAM President took their toll. At the peak, around 2005, I was constantly traveling and spent most of my time on the road or in the air. I also had the feeling that I had done what I could in the organic sector and that the concept of organic farming for bringing change had some severe limitations. Through market success and trying to be relevant by adjusting the narrative to mainstream agendas, the label organic had lost some of its transformative powers. The same market forces that drive large-scale farming and monocultures in conventional agriculture also became more visible in organic cultivation. This was observed already by some in the eighties, but lately the conventionalization of organic farming is the subject of many academic inquiries (ROVER ET AL 2022).

During this whole period, I was still living on the farm. I had, however, lost some of the engagement in it. This was also self-inflicted as I was convinced that it was those that actually did the work that should decide what work needs to be done and how to do it. During my many years of semi-absence, the farm had also embarked on new ventures, such as a jam-making business, which I was somewhat less interested in. Vegetable production had expanded considerably, adopting a large-scale and less diverse approach. This meant that we became structurally dependent on hired labor, which came with big implications. When you work for yourself, you still need to make ends meet, cover all your costs and pay your bills, as well as getting remuneration for the time spent. It is still up to you at any given time how you go about it, however. When you have hired a labor force you inevitably must focus on productivity and efficiency as the workers' salary has to be justified and carefully accounted for most of the time. You are also confronted with the fact that some people work well and others less so and that forces you to seek those with a better performance rate. Another aspect that changed with hiring labor was that our very informal way of management did not work since our employees were not present at the dinner table. In any case, they were more interested in clear management structures than participatory workplace democracy. At one point in time, we suggested that the jam-making business should be converted to a workers' cooperative, but the staff was not interested as they realized they would have to take on more responsibility and work harder but earn less.

I had the typical mid-life crisis. Questioning my purpose, what I had accomplished so far and how I had done it, as well as the relationship with my partner were just some of the things I struggled with. For almost half a year between 2007 and 2008, I took some time out. Bicycling my way across the Baltic states, Poland, Ukraine, Turkey, Greece, Italy, France and finally Switzerland, where time and money ran out. So, I hopped on a train home. Right after returning, I decided to move out of the farm. To this day, I miss the place itself, the companionship and the friendship.

From a young age, I was very interested in developments that look at the bigger picture as I was trying to understand what was wrong and what was good in the world. For more than 30 years, I have been involved in practical action, appropriate technology, organic farming, and other ways of making a change here and there with an emphasis on organizational work. I still think that is a commendable thing to do, but sometimes you also get a bit lost in the short-term issues. A case in point is my work linking smallholders to export markets. While this certainly increased their revenue, I did get less and less convinced that integration into often unreliable global markets was the best way forward for small farm development. Even though I do think it is great if someone can make at least a few hundred dollars more per year, in the end, there will be a limited number of well-resourced farmers that will reap the benefits.

> "Increasing exports of *high-value crops* primarily means further increasing imports of staple foods, which is a *risky strategy* and leads both farmers and countries away from *self-determination*."

During my trip, I started writing in an effort to summarize my view of the world. It resulted in the book Garden Earth—From Hunter and Gatherers to Global Capitalism and Thereafter, published in Swedish in 2010 and in English in 2012. In 2011, I wrote yet another book with my wife-to-be, Ann-Helen. This was followed by three more books, one on my own and two with Ann-Helen. The books look at modern civilization and its relationship to the natural world from different angles. Always with some kind of focus on food and agriculture, because it is my core area of expertise, and it is the most important way we interact with the rest of the natural world for better or worse.

In 2014, we bought a small farm outside of Uppsala. The plan was to mainly grow vegetables and plant fruit and nut trees on a smaller scale. The farm was a bit bigger than our plans were calling for. It covered 40 hectares of forested land and far more cropland than we needed. Most of the cropland was very low-lying, frequently flooded by the lake and in permanent grasslands. In the end, we realized that grazing and hay was the best way to use the land for food production. We restored some 10 hectares of former grassland that had been spontaneously reforested. In Sweden, semi-natural grasslands are hotspots for biodiversity, but in the last century at least ninety per cent has been abandoned, mostly converted to plantation forests of little value for biodiversity.

To manage the land, we bought some cows and established a small herd of mother cows with offspring. This coincided with a huge increase in veganism. The media portrayed cows as climate killers that are on par with, or even worse than, cars and airplanes. We considered that the scientific data had flaws as many claims were valid for only a certain type of livestock farming methods, but not for all. In addition, we realized that there was little understanding of the long-term partnership between man and cattle, sheep and other grazing animals, cultural values and the contribution to a sustainable food system. So, we wrote a book about cows, The Planet of the Cows, which was well received. The book was the result of us buying cows, which would have never happened, had we not bought that particular farm that allowed us to do it. In the end, it is all thanks to a chain reaction caused by a series of coincidences.

Our latest book, The Living, was published in 2023. It too was inspired by a specific event. We started writing it after participating in the public debate about food, agriculture, forestry and the environment. We realized that in the view of some, all human use of nature is by definition harmful. This means that the way forward is to limit this as much as possible. This would include the ban of producing food in industrial processes, the keeping

Fig. 4: Apple tree rootstock in nursery at the Sunnansjö farm in Sweden

Fig. 5: Delivering a speech at the Biofach fair in Nuremberg

of livestock and firewood, to name a few. The majority, though, regard nature as a mine to be extracted and are convinced that we can find technological solutions to all the problems we have created, preferably with market mechanisms. This means that there are underlying assumptions and worldviews that need to be brought into the open and discussed. It is only then that we can have a meaningful conversation about farming, biodiversity, and the climate. We promote a view of an interactive relationship between humanity and any living thing. Our lives should be geared towards positive contributions to biodiversity. Parallel to writing books, Ann-Helen works as a journalist and I have given a considerable number of lectures and worked as an independent consultant, mostly taking jobs in Sweden. Both of us are still very much active on the farm and work on further developing it.

Based on my experience with Torfolk, the organic market, small holders in Africa and the general development of the food market, I have come to the conclusion that the market mechanism itself is problematic as it reduces food and agriculture to products to be sold and the land itself to a commodity. On our farm, we want to implement a relational approach instead of a transactional one as a leading principle, putting the focus on the relationship between the consumer and us, the producers. Since we as farmers are in close contact with the ones that consume on the one hand and on the other hand have to form an alliance with nature in order to feed us, we believe that philosophically speaking, food is an expression of these relationships. The meat we produce is all sold directly to consumers, many of whom live close by and can see our cows. The vegetables are sold in Reko-rings (ISAKSSON ET AL 2020) and Ann-Helen is an administrator of one of them in Uppsala. Torfolk, my first farm, has moved into that direction too now. Instead of using the market as a tool to change things for the better such as with organic certification, this strategy aims to reduce the power of the market and replace it with relationships, even if money is still part of the exchange. In addition, we want to develop other non-market

> "If you believe, like I do, that capitalism as a system is harmful, that *food and agriculture should be accessible* to all members of society and that humanity should make room for other species, while at the same time be a responsible keystone species, then you probably agree with me that the short-, and medium-term actions, including political demands, should contribute to *the reality you desire*."

mechanisms based on produce as commons (RUNDGREN 2016, VIVERO-POL 2017). Lately, we have started to give food to a charity for homeless people. We are able to do this now due to having multiple streams of income, including the pension I have been getting for the past two years.

Clearly, it should have become evident by now, everything I have applied myself to, every path I have followed, has not been that straightforward. It all just kind of happened as I went along. As soon as something popped up that needed urgent attention, I committed to it. A bit like a Renaissance man, I have dabbled in and mastered skills all across the board, including physical labor as well as organizational, intellectual and analytical projects. I guess that reflects my personality. I am also more of an entrepreneur than a steward despite my theoretical affiliation to stewardship and critical view of the restless innovation and creative destruction nowadays. The latter expression has been first described by Schumpeter in 1942. In theory, I am a stern proponent of

community building, through trust and relationships, despite being an introvert. Therefore, on a personal level, I am just not so keen on interacting much with other people, it is exhausting.

I do not have a change theory, but I have strong misgivings about so many of the ways both society and organizations are managing, or trying to manage, change today, where setting goals and strategic plans are seen as major tools. This approach affects personal life, such as setting one's own professional goals as well as anything on a global scale like the Paris Agreement and the Sustainable Development Goals. Setting ambitious long-term goals concerning climate change policies seems to mainly be an excuse for doing very little in the short term. Development projects have been dominated by the latest planning tools. I have spent many hours developing logical frameworks (EU 2023) and reporting accordingly. Businesses and organizations have spent endless energy on standardized ISO 9000 quality assurance with limited value (RUNDGREN 2012).

For sure, there are certain things that are best accomplished by setting goals, like the moon landing or graduating from an educational program. Plans and goals are useful but can only be used as short-term guidelines. They need to be regularly revised to accommodate changes in the environment. Their main value lies in making people reflect on the methods and the reasons they approach anything they do, rather than just zeroing in on the end result. In general, personal or social developments do not work in a planned manner. I believe it is more interesting to be flexible and to follow certain principles, values and processes than sticking to certain goals and plans.

It is also important to realize that humanity is not as much in control as we think. Many developments are caused by changes in an external environment. This means that adaptability and resilience are very important characteristics on a personal, organizational and societal level. Timing is often critical when it comes to change. Some things may seem impossible at a certain time, but might be possible, or even necessary, all of a sudden. Launching KRAV happened at the right time. As timing is difficult and cannot be planned, we were lucky in this regard. This means that a certain opportunism is crucial.

When designing strategies for change, it is important to work with methods and means that include ultimate targets. If you believe, like I do, that capitalism as a system is harmful, that food and agriculture should be accessible to all members of society and that humanity should make room for other species, while at the same time be a responsible keystone species, then you probably agree with me that the short-, and medium-term actions, including political demands, should contribute to the reality you desire. Take market instruments like carbon credits for example. In regard to combating climate change, they certainly might have some short-term benefits as they are simple and can easily be implemented in marketing frameworks. However, such strategies will increase the influence of capitalism and lead to commodification of even more parts of the relationship between humans and nature, which is exactly the opposite of the development we desire. Self-provisioning and self-sufficiency of communities lead to less consumption, hence less emissions. It reduces the time available for salaried employment, thus shrinking the economy and ultimately human pressure on ecosystems. Turning this into political demands is part of a strategy that makes downsizing and moving away from capitalism possible. The context might be different but thinking about his essay Reform and Revolution from 1968 for instance, I cannot help but see a ton of similarities with André Gorz. This will significantly change our culture and people's mindset as well as inspire new forms of self-management and democracy. It can be done here and now.

REFERENCES

EU 2023 = Logical Framework Approach, https://wikis.ec.europa.eu/display/ExactExternalWiki/Logical+Framework+Approach+-+LFA [30/12/2023]

GORZ ANDRÉ 1968 = Gorz, André (1968) Reform and Revolution, Vol. 5: Socialist Register 1968

IFOAM 2023 = https://www.ifoam.bio/why-organic/shaping-agriculture/four-principles-organic [07/03/2024]

IFOAM 2024 = The Organic Guarantee System of IFOAM, https://www.ifoam.bio/our-work/how/standards-certification/organic-guarantee-system [07/03/2024]

ISAKSSON ET AL 2020 = Isaksson, Filippa/ Leijon Cedermark, Marie (2020) Opportunities for Short Food Supply Chains : attractive communication strategies within a Swedish REKO-ring

ROVER ET AL 2020 = Rover, Oscar José/ da Silva Pugas, Adevan/ De Gennaro, Bernardo Corrado/ Vittori, Francesco/ Roselli, Luigi (2020) Conventionalization of Organic Agriculture: A Multiple Case Study Analysis in Brazil and Italy. Sustainability 2020, 12, 6580. https://doi.org/10.3390/su12166580 [07/03/2024]

RUNDGREN 2008 = Rundgren, Gunnar (2008) Organic Exports, a way to a better life, EPOPA 2008, 110 pages http://www.grolink.se/epopa/Publications/Epopa-end-book.pdf [07/03/2024]

RUNDGREN 2012 = Rundgren, Gunnar (2012) Quality management is a management fad elevated to divinity, The Organic Standard Issue 138, https://www.researchgate.net/publication/315113707_A_management_fad_elevated_to_divinity [07/03/2024]

RUNDGREN 2016 = Rundgren, Gunnar (2016) Food: From Commodity to Commons. J Agric Environ Ethics 29, 103–121 (2016). https://doi.org/10.1007/s10806-015-9590-7 [07/03/2024]

SCHUMPETER 1942 = Schumpeter, Joseph (1942) Capitalism, Socialism, and Democracy (1942), Harper & Brothers.

UN 2023 = THE 17 GOALS, https://sdgs.un.org/goals [30/12/2023]

Vivero-Pol 2017 = Vivero-Pol, José Luis (2017) Food as Commons or Commodity? Exploring the Links between Normative Valuations and Agency in Food Transition. Sustainability 2017, 9, 442. https://doi.org/10.3390/su9030442 [07/03/2024]

A conversation between Stella Rollig & Karl Stocker

Art As Tool For
Emancipation

STELLA ROLLIG has been General Director and Scientific Director of the Belvedere Museum in Vienna since January 2017. She studied German literature and art history at the University of Vienna and worked as an art journalist. From 1994 to 1996 Stella Rollig was the Austrian Federal Curator for Fine Arts, during which time she also founded Depot – Kunst und Diskussion in the MuseumsQuartier Vienna. From 2004 to 2016, she headed the art museum Lentos in Linz after working as an exhibition organizer for many years. In addition to her curatorial activities, Stella Rollig has taught at numerous institutes, including the Academy of Fine Arts Munich, the University of Art and Industrial Design Linz and the ZHdK Zurich University of the Arts. Stella Rollig has been a member of many juries.

(K S) **Let us start with a very personal question. What made you get involved with art? How did you get into art? Why did you take this path?**

(S R) Art has never been foreign to me in my life. I come from a middle-class family in which an interest in art and culture was to be expected and considered good manners, so to speak. Part of this was that on the weekends, parents took their kids to museums from an early age and then also dropped them off at the museum's children's workshop. I felt at home in the world of museums, it was familiar to me. Our parents encouraged and taught us how to read works of art, how to interpret them. That was a relatively gentle introduction, which of course was not always too welcome either, but essentially integral to everyday life.

Later, I decided to study literature because linguistics and writing were very important to me. I have always wanted to write. As a teenager I thought about becoming a novelist, but in the end, I considered applied writing like journalism a more suitable profession. Subsequently I realized that art, due to its complexity, its depth and the surprise factor, has the ability to inspire my mind in such a way that it was the most amazing challenge to do it justice using language.

Concerning my professional and personal development, I maintained acquaintances and friendships after being introduced to artists, which is how I moved from the world of museums to contemporary art because you have to get familiarized with it somehow, and that is exactly what happened while I was at university. During my German studies, I slowly started exploring and looking into art academies, a much more tempting milieu than the structured and obedient social environment I was usually surrounded

Fig. 1: Visitors to the Upper Belvedere

by. That is how I got to know artists of my generation and eventually went from art critic to curator. Something I never wanted was to become an art broker, educator or a manager, because at heart, I do not have a strong sense of mission where I would feel the need to spread a particular message. I do not want to have to convince anyone of anything they do not believe in or persuade people of the importance of art.

In any case, I come from a non-institutional position. I worked as a freelancer for many years of my professional life. Here I should perhaps mention the period in which I was the Austrian federal curator, where I had a large budget at my disposal from the Minister of Culture to promote

56

contemporary art in Austria, at a time, in the early and mid-nineties, when I was fully convinced that compelling art could only take place outside institutions. The focus of my work at that time was on facilitating public art, performances and campaigns in urban areas as well as empowering self-organized creative art spaces and projects.

A great influence on my attitude toward art and my concept of it was the institutional critique as it emerged from the emancipatory movements, the Women's Rights Movement, and the Civil Rights Movement in the United States of America, leading to the establishment of activist groups such as the Art Workers' Coalition. At that time, my focus was very much US-centric, and I was fascinated by the art that was being created in North America and mesmerized by the art scenes themselves, especially in New York and Los Angeles.

> **"I have learned to understand art as a tool of *emancipation* in the broadest sense, thus not only speaking for *women*, but in regard to positions of *all minorities.*"**

I wanted to dedicate my work to that. It undoubtedly did come from a sense of defiance. Back then, I would have never dreamt of becoming a museum director, especially since I am neither an art historian with an academic degree, nor have I ever graduated in German studies.

But then suddenly, I became a museum director. I am always worried that it sounds a bit smug. Truthfully speaking, I did not think that my experience and knowledge were appropriate and fitting in the museum sector. Nonetheless, I was approached and encouraged to apply right after the founding director of the Lentos Museum in Linz retired just one year after reopening. I was truly flattered and excited to take on such a great responsibility. Yet on the spur of a moment, I, an avid advocate of the institutional critique, was the head of an institution. However, I do think that to this day, this has helped me immensely to implement as well as ardently advocate for ideas of change, even nowadays at the Belvedere.

K S On that account, is it possible to make a difference in the institutions after all?

S R You can make a difference, yes. For me personally, as someone who was hired for a job without any prior qualifications and experience in that area, there were two aspects, two sides of the same coin. On the one hand, I was quite idealistic and driven by the desire to make a change, which in fact I managed to do a few times. On the other hand, I had no clue about most of the requirements that come with running a museum. Namely the loan network, the insurance policies, restorations and so on. That was new to me, and today I am beginning to realize that I probably put my foot in my mouth a few times without even noticing it. Human resources management within an institution was another subject I had to learn from scratch when I started working there. At Lentos—in addition to this responsibility, I started leading the Nordico City Museum in 2011—I was supervising about 40 employees. Compare this to the Belvedere, where we are ten times as many staff members. Today there are about 350 employees with a budget that is more than ten times as large. By the time I changed roles, I had already picked up on the essential structures and mechanisms. In both cases, the leadership role primarily

Fig. 2: Exterior view of the Upper Belvedere

ART AS TOOL FOR EMANCIPATION

> "Rooted in my experience as a journalist, I reckon it is less interesting how a picture is painted rather than in what *circumstances* it was created, what is its *intention*, what *insights* does it offer, how did the artist do during this time—in other words, to considering and including the overall *societal context* of the picture."

implies making decisions and solving problems. Unfortunately, a lot of other things fall by the wayside, like writing, free, wild creativity and, above all, the closeness to the artists—I miss it all.

K S But you are simply becoming more of an enabler, even though you can hardly curate art by yourself now, but you can inspire and drive innovation, you can assist and support, you have the ability to delegate projects in a way that they get done. And I believe that is a quality that your staff might appreciate about you. Assuming you would not be one to complain about their work shortly before the opening.

S R Rarely—sometimes I do regret that I do not do it though. However, concerning the work on any of the exhibitions, it is extremely important to me that my standards are met. I am pretty fussy and meticulous about that.

I have a curatorial team of 20 to 25 people, and we collaborate on creating the concept of the exhibition program. That is up to 20 special exhibitions in one year across all three locations of the Belvedere, ranging from medieval art to the latest contemporary. My expertise lies in art created in the present, therefore I am not an expert on most of the art we collect and show. I see my role in conveying my idea of what an interesting exhibition is. What is a theme even? What is worth telling? Art historians often have a different perception of an intriguing theme than I do. Rooted in my experience as a journalist, I reckon it is less interesting how a picture is painted rather than in what circumstances it was created, what is its intention, what insights does it offer, how did the artist do during this time—in other words, considering and including the overall societal context of the picture. There is no way around discussing this every single time.

K S But that is classic high culture, is it not?

S R Yes, if you want to stick to that category. However, at Belvedere 21, our location for contemporary art, we have an open, interdisciplinary public program and numerous participatory and collaborative projects as part of the Community Outreach program. In 2018, we were the first national museum to hire our own curator for community outreach, Christiane Erharter. Since then, we have seen marvelous projects egressing from the scene

Fig. 3: Lena Henke, Aldo Rossi's Sleeping Elephant, 2018

while being developed discretely. Christiane and the curators of contemporary art are in constant contact with artists and develop and produce programs together: performances, movie nights at the in-house cinema Blicke or project presentations.

K S This entertains a side of you that you have always liked to live yourself.

S R Yes, but as irony would have it, I can hardly participate due to time constraints and only hear about how most of these events went from reports and see it in our records. And I always think to myself, amazing, a lot of people showed up and had fun, how awesome that was.

K S But that suggests that everything at your museum is covered, the experimentation, coming up with new things, evaluating where everything is supposed to be headed?

S R Yes, for sure. I will probably witness a handover to the next generation that I have not fully gotten to know yet. In Linz, I personally went to every artist-run space and every art studio and arranged projects with the artists. Despite all my numerous tasks as director, I insisted on keeping this up. But as the general director of a large national museum, there is not enough time anymore. And to be honest, I am not up for every single party anymore.

K S For that matter, your current position fits rather well then, does it not? I think that biographies are designed in such a way that one constantly develops, consequently leading up to a point where one makes decisions about the future, whether you want that or not. There are many people who get into a position that they do not really want to be in because they would much rather continue what they were doing before. Additionally, further interesting topics gradually crop up, of course.

S R I agree with you. You have to want such a position, with all its aspects. I understand people who prefer being curators to running a museum. I was always curious about new challenges, about learning. What guarantees stability today and my work a solid perspective—as well as serenity—is based on my preoccupation with the history of the museum as an institution.

In 2023, the Belvedere celebrated its three-hundredth anniversary, referring to the completion of the Upper Belvedere in 1723. In the seventeen-eighties, the Upper Belvedere was one of the first public museums in the world. The Imperial Picture Gallery, as it was called at the time, was open to the public for free admission a few days a week and anyone could come and look at the paintings. We still feel connected to this historical foundation in our inclusive attitude today.

The most interesting insight from looking back on the past 300 years was that the museum is an extremely strong institution. You and I both adopted Foucault's ideas, who analyzed and deconstructed the fundamental institutions of the state and identified them as instruments of discipline and control. The museum is one of them. But Foucault has also concurred that these establishments, that according to him also comprise of educational institutions, hospitals and prisons, maintain a certain social structure that especially now seems to be very threatened. I am convinced that the museum as an organization, not only manages, but moreover preserves cultural heritage, thereupon having an obligation to showcase and conserve it for future generations while not forgetting to constantly re-evaluate and contextualize anything in its possession.

> "Considering all the disasters that struck between 1780 and 2024, the museum has essentially *survived all these hardships* well."

This provides an indispensable basis for all necessary discourses on origin and identity. Identity politics use museums as a platform to depict and further develop their discourses—as critical as they may be and should be. This is a museum's raison d'être, which will not change despite our immensely crisis-ridden here and now and, judging from today's perspective, very gloomy future.

Upon taking a closer look, due to the museum's vulnerability in combination with a strong call for finding solutions to conflicts it is supposed to create space for while at the same time feeling the pressure of having to meet certain expectations, it is a prime example for an utterly overwhelmed institution.

K S Can you give me some indicators concerning this?

S R In some respects, the subjects and works of museums have never been as potentially explosive as of now. For

Fig. 4: Stella Rollig in conversation with Alois Mosbacher in the artist's studio

Fig. 5: Community Outreach program at Belvedere 21, 2020

instance, let us look at the planning of exhibitions. From one point of view, contemporary art and art history are increasingly to be shown and displayed in reference to their global dimension. Yet, there is a justified focus on the ecological imperative demanding a more sustainable process in light of climate change and its devastating effects. We know that loans from overseas, like works of art that are temporarily flown in for exhibitions, are among the worst causes for climate change. This means that we have to fundamentally rethink fairly old guidelines on organizing exhibits. Sooner or later, I presume there will be a split from the idea that exhibitions can only be considered excellent and worthy when they include originals and that reproductions are reserved for embarrassing events at third-rate exhibition venues.

In other respects: The comprehensive digital transformation requires enormous resources. The legal requirements for anything you have to take care of at a museum, such as contracts and rights clearances, are becoming increasingly complicated, as are safety regulations. Bureaucracy and hedging are undoubtedly intensifying.

K S How do you deal with contemporary criticism of museums?

S R I was very indignant about some of the criticism when we had to close the museums at the height of the

Covid pandemic and we were struggling so much, especially the previously incredibly successful museums, financially speaking. Deep down, I realized from one day to the next that I no longer saw any point in the work of museums. If there is no audience, then who are you doing all this for? At this point, an entirely unnecessary discussion broke out, which insinuated that the successful museums were just tailored towards tourists and neglected the local visitors. Over and over, I have replied, yes, the Belvedere is tremendously popular with foreign visitors, but that is not a bad thing at all, in fact it is genuinely exciting to cater to such a diverse crowd of museumgoers. We have to keep in mind that guests from South Korea—which was our strongest group of visitors before the pandemic—as well as kids from a Viennese middle school should feel engaged and inspired when they come here. Of course, there is a lot to criticize about the museum as an institution, and no museum is perfect, but I take credit for the fact that I am a very self-critical director. And these accusations did not really understand the crucial points.

K S Which would be?

S R Admitting that the museum is overwhelmed in some respects and that according to the philosophy of marketing and competition, it is not allowed to disclose that. No museum can meet all requests concerning diversification and inclusion, political statements, solutions, service, science and entertainment. Let us acknowledge this and rethink the tasks of museums.

K S What keeps you optimistic? What is your optimism based on?

S R My optimism is grounded in achievements that have worked out time and again. Which brings us back to our topic: change processes. You can change the attitude, frame of reference and mindset of an institution, referring to its employees. I prefer to work with people who think critically and not affirmatively. I love that, in my mid-sixties, I am being overtaken in my critical consciousness by my co-workers, who could be my children. That is wonderful. They are truly woke, and they do point out blind spots in my own perception or my approach. I see a lot of vigor, novelty, and a keen social awareness in a new generation of museum directors. The desire I have always had to refuse to openly address problems and doubts about the institution, and to facilitate discussions about the museum as an institute, is increasingly considered the norm among younger generations. Not feeling the need to just advertise and sell your museum's projects and your work—everything is fantastic, and everything is extraordinary. The younger ones are somehow more relaxed.

Fig. 6: Visitors to the Upper Belvedere in front of Gustav Klimt's "The Kiss"

Words by   Pier Paolo Peruccio

Design And *Complexity*

PIER PAOLO PERUCCIO holds a PhD in Architecture. He is a Full Professor of Design at the Polytechnic University of Turin in Italy and a Visiting Professor at the Campus of the Technological Institute of Monterrey in Mexico City. He develops research in the areas of design history, environmental sustainability, and innovation. He is a design historian with an approach to design that is connected to history—understood not only as a discipline oriented toward interpreting sources, but as a means to be able to aim for innovation in the future with more effective tools and greater awareness. He is the Scientific Director of the Editoriale Domus' worldesign magazine, the founder and Director of the SYDERE—Systemic Design Research and Education—Center and has been a member of the board of directors of several organizations such as the World Design Organization from 2019 to 2023, the Italian Scientific Society of Design from 2021 to 2024, as of 2020, the PLART Foundation, and since 2018, the Aurelio Peccei Foundation.

DESIGN AND COMPLEXITY

P P In this brief article, I will analyze five keywords that I believe are fundamental to understanding the more complex and tangible aspects of design practice today. These are words I have pondered over the past 25 years while directing design magazines such as worldesign, Il Giornale del Design, and AIS Design History of Design, as well as teaching it at the Polytechnic University of Turin in Italy, the Technological Institute of Monterrey in Mexico, and the Tongji University in China among others.

Additionally, I reflected on these concepts while serving as a board member in decision-making processes for international institutions such as the International Council of Societies of Industrial Design, ICSID, the World Design Organization, WDO, and the Italian Design Society as a jury member for prestigious awards, including the iF Award in Germany, the Compasso d'Oro in Italy, the Golden Pin Design Award in Taiwan, and the Confederation of Indian Institute Design Excellence Awards.

1 The first keyword, perhaps unsurprisingly, is design. It is a word that often raises more questions than it answers, prompting every speaker to spend a few moments at the beginning of each discussion clarifying the scope of the designer's role. Rarely have I witnessed any consensus on the meaning of this term. We can almost say that every designer—and perhaps every individual—has their own interpretation. This variation stems from the fact that the discipline is still relatively young and lacks a definitive, universally accepted definition. Despite this, it is increasingly attracting public attention, and at long last, has become central to policy discussions in certain countries. Notably in Europe, design is at the heart of numerous projects funded through initiatives such as the New European Bauhaus, Social Innovation, and Circular Economy programs.

Within this field, I find two definitions particularly representative, as they capture the essence of the discipline. The first one calls it a catalyst for change—an agent that accelerates and facilitates reactions within a system thus enabling desired transformations to take shape. In this sense, design functions as a powerful engine that drives innovation and brings tangible changes to reality.

The second definition, which is broader in scope, focuses on the role and function of design as a practice that is activated every time we intervene in the real world through concrete actions. This intervention follows a specific approach, characterized by a clear, structured sequence of operational phases. However, it is important to emphasize that these methodological steps are not limited to the formal beginning of a project. In fact, there is often an ongoing and underlying preparatory phase, during which design accumulates somewhat semi-finished elements of innovation. This process represents a kind of cognitive and creative sedimentation, where every experience, observation, or reflection contributes to a growing knowledge and insight base that will later translate into design actions.

In essence, design is not confined to specific moments of conscious intervention but is a continuous process that manifests each time we alter reality. Every action, every decision—even in the most everyday contexts—carries a design dimension. In this sense, we can say that we are designing constantly, either explicitly or implicitly, endlessly collecting elements that fuel our design efforts. This ongoing dialogue between thought and action creates fertile ground for innovation and the transformation of the context in which we operate.

Fig. 1: Chairing the Research and Education Forum, WDO General Assembly, Tokyo, October 2023

② The second keyword I consider essential for describing the contemporary context is complexity. This term is often referenced when examining crises—ranging from environmental and health issues to geopolitical and migratory crises.

The word itself, derived from the Latin root complexus, meaning "woven together", captures the multifaceted and interconnected problematic nature of current challenges. Complexity, in its essence, suggests that phenomena are not isolated but intertwined, often influencing each other in intricate ways. The term gained considerable prominence starting in the sixties, as it contrasts with simplicity. In Edgar Morin's view, complexity refers to the uncertainty faced by the observer when analyzing phenomena, which often leads to reducing or oversimplifying the activity.

The difficulty in managing design projects, for example, has led architects and designers toward the rationalization of the design process, a topic that remains widely debated, especially in design schools. Christopher Alexander's book titled Notes on the Synthesis of Form from 1964 arose from the need to equip this process with new methodological tools to address the emerging complexities.

Today, everything seems intricately interconnected, making it impossible to disentangle and separate the issues underlying contemporary crises. These challenges are systemic by nature and require a holistic approach rather than a segmented one. The environmental issue, for example, cannot be resolved through a reductionist method of inquiry. Instead, it is crucial to adopt an approach based on systems thinking—one that focuses on relationships, and the study of systems, subsystems, and the connections between them. The Earth, after all, should be viewed as a set of continuously changing behavioral configurations, as highlighted in the first report to the Club of Rome, The Limits to Growth (MEADOWS / MEADOWS / RANDERS / BEHRENS 1972).

This volume, published in 1972, is based on modeling the world system, a sort of contemporary digital twin. It analyzes the interaction of five critical factors—population, food production, industrialization, pollution, and exploitation of natural resources—using the system dynamics approach, with the aid of MIT computers in Cambridge, Massachusetts. Although not the author, Aurelio Peccei is the key

Fig. 2: The U.S.-Mexico border fence at the Tijuana beach, 2024

> "Today's major issues—from the climate crisis to food scarcity, poverty, the green transition, and migration—commonly referred to as *big global challenges*, should not be tackled with a *reductionist approach*."

figure associated with the book. Peccei was one of the founders of the Club of Rome, an informal, apolitical, and independent think tank now known for promoting The Limits to Growth report.

Aurelio Peccei, an executive at Olivetti, FIAT, and one of the founders of Alitalia, had a clear understanding that all phenomena are interrelated. He recognized that significant methodological effort is required to manage the world problematique. In a letter written shortly after the Club of Rome's first meeting in 1968, Peccei remarked that "there is a growing number of problems facing humanity, which are of a complex and multivariant character [...] at present, we lack sufficient understanding of these problems." (PECCEI 1968). This web of difficulties is referred to by the Club of Rome as the problematique—a complex tangle where it is challenging to isolate secluded problems or propose individual solutions. These interwoven issues grow at an exponential rate, with their severity often going unnoticed until it is too late to change course.

Today's major issues—from the climate crisis to food scarcity, poverty, the green transition, and migration—commonly referred to as big global challenges, should not be tackled with a reductionist approach. Instead, they must be examined through a systemic lens. Even Don Norman, in his latest book Design for a Better World from 2023, advocates for adopting a systems thinking approach.

3 This brings us to the third keyword, system. This term is widely used today, just as it was in the sixties, as Ludwig von Bertalanffy observed in his book General System Theory from 1968. He noted its spread across various fields of science, language, and media. As a concept that transcends multiple disciplines, it has been broadly adopted across various contexts with few major modifications. In design, for instance, terms like resilience, autopoiesis, and homeostasis are frequently used, sometimes with limited precision. However, it is the relationships within systems that take on a crucial role in systems thinking. These form the foundation for a paradigm shift capable of altering interactions among numerous actors from a non-reductionist perspective.

The well-known saying "the whole is more than the sum of its parts" emphasizes the idea that a system possesses qualities that individual parts, even when combined, cannot achieve. It is composed of elements that, when organized together, produce outcomes that exceed the capabilities of each part alone.

According to Donella H. Meadows, one of the authors of The Limits to Growth, a system must satisfy three conditions. These include the presence of elements, the connections between them, and a specific purpose. She uses the metaphor of the digestive system to illustrate this idea. It consists of teeth, enzymes, the stomach, and intestines, all working together to convert food into nutrients that are absorbed into the bloodstream. Similarly, a soccer team, made up of players, a coach, the field, and the ball, all connected through the game's rules and the coach's strategy, functions as one too. The goal might be to win, have fun, or make money. A school, a city, or a forest can also be seen as a system, as can something much larger like the Earth, the solar system, or even a galaxy. Furthermore, systems can be nested within larger ones.

When there are only disconnected parts without relationships, it is not considered a system but rather a set. In such cases, the properties of a set do not change if elements are added or removed. A system, however, is not a tangible object but a conceptual representation that exists only in our minds. Its boundaries are arbitrarily defined by the observer—based on their knowledge objective.

ⓘ WHAT IS SYSTEMS THINKING?

Systems thinking is defined as contextual thinking, as it considers the object of analysis as part of a network of relationships embedded in a larger network. It is process-oriented, spanning multiple disciplines—from biology to chemistry, economics to philosophy, psychology to mathematics, and even architecture to design. The concept of systems thinking has historical roots, with the first term evolving over centuries. From Heraclitus and Giambattista Vico to the twentieth century, the idea expanded through advancements in modern physics, investigations into atomic and subatomic realms, and connections to holistic perspectives culturally close to certain Eastern religions and ancient philosophies.

Systems thinking, with its broad perspective, allows us to understand the interconnections between elements and to see the entire framework. It also provides a more focused view, enabling us to discern finer details and granular components within the structure.

Fig. 3: Playa de Tijuana, the beach where the border fence goes into the ocean

④ Another key term closely tied to the previous concepts is behavior, especially in the context of design, such as behavioral design or design for behavioral change.

Over the past twenty years, design has emerged as a fundamental catalyst for social improvement, particularly in urban environments. It plays a significant role in shaping behaviors and contributing to individual well-being. These aspects, which were relatively unexplored until the nineties, have become central to academic and professional discussions in design.

Furthermore, design has expanded its scope, now encompassing a wide range of diverse disciplines. Today, design studios collaborate with anthropologists, geographers, philosophers and other experts in various fields, reflecting Tim Brown's idea that it has become too important to be left solely to designers. Including professionals from these diverse fields leads to richer perspectives and effective solutions. It is beneficial to have psychologists, cognitive ergonomists, and philosophers at the table, alongside engineers and architects, who have traditionally represented a different side of design. This collaborative approach can be applied in the design of smart districts, where tools like user manuals provide tips for small behavioral changes. These manuals explain how to use the components, systems, and services within an apartment, as well as across an entire complex or district. The goal is to address everyday problems while raising awareness about the benefits and impacts of our daily choices.

The Smart Life Book is a manual conceived, designed, and developed for Euromilano that translates the complexity of the architectural project into an accessible guide, helping users utilize their homes correctly and efficiently (PERUCCIO / SAVINA / VIGLIOGLIA 2019). One section is dedicated to conscious living, guiding users through an understanding of the structural and system design of the residences. Specifically, it provides a straightforward analysis of each component's characteristics and functionality, enabling users to understand how these various devices work together to meet functional needs like heating, cooling, supplying electricity, water, and insulation. The home is explained using systems thinking, which aims to provide detailed knowledge to a broad range of users from diverse backgrounds. This understanding is essential for raising user awareness about the resource consumption linked to their daily choices, while also providing users with alternative solutions.

5   The final key concept is the term "wall," which encompasses both physical and psychological boundaries, and extends metaphorically to disciplinary divides. Presently, walls are a focal point in discussions across the globe, symbolizing pressing geopolitical conflicts such as those between Russia and Ukraine, or Israel and Gaza. Beyond these political implications, the notion of walls plays a significant role in the design discourse, as exemplified by initiatives associated with San Diego and Tijuana World Design Capital 2024.

While serving on the board of directors of the World Design Organization, I observed the presentation of the San Diego and Tijuana bid. This bid highlighted a unique culture of cross-border collaboration and emphasized the transformative power of innovation in building a more interconnected, binational community.

"The selection of San Diego and Tijuana as *World Design Capitals* was a groundbreaking achievement for the organization, marking the first time the title was awarded to two cities *across national boundaries*."

The bid incorporated the concept of nepantla, a Nahuatl term meaning "in between," to characterize the interdependence of these two metropolitan economies. Rather than seeing San Diego and Tijuana as competitors, the bid framed them—along with their larger regional context including California and Baja California—as complementary regions. With a combined population of 7.1 million, one side thrives with high-tech industries, while the other is home to a robust manufacturing and service sector.

A wall physically divides these cities, forming a small segment of the larger 3,200-kilometer border that separates the United States from Mexico. This wall also

PIER PAOLO PERUCCIO

Fig. 4: Cover and internal pages of The Smart Life Book, 2019

The topics of walls, artifacts, and migration were investigated in the exhibition Arqueología en Tránsito, Archeology in Transit, curated by José de la O and myself. The exhibition was held in Tijuana, Mexico, and San Diego, United States of America, during two Design Weeks in 2024—in Tijuana on May 4 and 5 and in San Diego from September 19 to September 25. The project employed a collaborative design research strategy, involving researchers from the Technological Institute of Monterrey, including a visiting professor from the campus in Mexico City during the first semester of 2024. The research spanned across various Mexican territories, from Chiapas to Chihuahua, collecting and analyzing artifacts that reflect the migrant experience. As philosopher Giorgio Agamben wrote in the opening of his essay Creation and Anarchy in 2017, "Archaeology is the only way to access the present".

This research and exhibition examined the connection between individuals and artifacts as a key lens to understand migration complexities. Using generative, co-creative workshops, participants selected and analyzed artifacts, ranging from modified plastic bottles to symbolic items, transforming them into focal points for stories about migration and borders. The exhibition encouraged reflection on modern global borders, where rise in physical barriers paradoxically coincides with increased migration and conflict. It emphasized how objects, as silent companions in migration journeys, can deepen our understanding, and suggested that archaeological studies of artifacts can inform and improve the design process.

The Archeology in Transit project delved into the complex relationship between human experiences and the objects that bear witness to them, contributing to conversations around migration,

symbolically divides the Global South from the Global North, underscoring the contrast between emerging and established economies. These terms, which originated in the sixties in response to socio-economic issues, have since evolved to address contemporary challenges, especially the climate crisis. As Arturo Escobar elaborates in Design for the Pluriverse, they now represent two distinct frameworks for approaching transition discourse. In the Global North, the dominant models include degrowth, transition towns, and circular economies. In contrast, the Global South tends to emphasize perspectives rooted in buen vivir and post-development frameworks.

cultural heritage, and resilience. The exhibition highlighted design and research's role in fostering empathy toward global issues. This theme proved especially relevant as Mexico undergoes significant shifts in migration dynamics. Once a country of emigration, Mexico now faces notable internal migration, as changes in economic, social, and political factors have transformed migration patterns. Notably, the flow of migrants now includes more women and children, many from previously stable regions.

This project emphasizes, from an academic perspective, how the archaeological analysis of objects can significantly enhance the design process by revealing the broader influence that functional items may have. For designers, it is crucial to consider not only a product's practical utility but also its capacity for emotional resonance, aiming to deepen the overall user experience. Today, over 80 borders exist globally, many of which have been established in the last two decades. Despite the proliferation of these barriers, migration flows and conflicts have only escalated. The artifacts displayed in this context—symbols of both human suffering and resilience—serve as reminders of humanity's deep-rooted history with boundaries, dating back to the first recorded walls of Jericho 12,000 years ago. Terms such as "barrier," "wall," "fence," and "fortification" often evoke themes of division and fear, particularly in the era post September 11, and have become even more significant in recent years. Thus, the theme of this exhibition remains deeply relevant. Objects, once silent witnesses, now emerge as narrators of human struggle, taking on central roles in the complex story of migration.

REFERENCES

AGAMBEN 2017 = Agamben, Agamben (2017) Creazione e anarchia: L'opera nell'età della religione capitalistica. Milano: Neri Pozza

ALEXANDER 1964 = Alexander, Christopher (1964) Notes on the synthesis of form. Cambridge: Harvard University Press

BERTALANFFY 1968 = Bertalanffy, Ludvig Von (1968) General System Theory, Foundations, Development, Applications, New York: George Braziller

ESCOBAR 2018 = Escobar, Arturo (2018) Designs for the Pluriverse: Radical Interdependence, Autonomy, and the Making of Worlds, Durham: Duke University Press

MEADOWS / MEADOWS / RANDERS / BEHRENS 1972 = Meadows, Dennis/ Meadows, Donella/ Randers, Jørgen/ Behrens, William III. (1972) The limits to Growth, New York: Universe Books

NORMAN 2023 = Norman, Donald (2023) Design for a better world, Meaningful, Sustainable, Humanity Centered, Cambridge: MIT Press.

PECCEI 1968 = Peccei, Aurelio (1968) Typewritten letter from Aurelio Peccei to Franco Archibugi, April 19, 1968, p.1, Turin: Agnelli Foundation Archive

PERUCCIO / SAVINA / VIGLIOGLIA 2019 = Peruccio, Pier Paolo/ Savina, Alessandra/ Viglioglia, Massimiliano (2019) The Smart Life Book. Uno strumento per conoscere, manutenere e sfruttare l'efficienza del sistema casa secondo principi sostenibili. Milano: Euromilano

Words by   Marsha Music

Detroit— Invisibility In The *Magnificent City*

MARSHA BATTLE PHILPOT, also known as Marsha Music, is an author and cultural historian, weaving structural analysis and personal narratives together in non-fiction works and in numerous anthologies. Her multidisciplinary practice focuses on the illumination of demographic shifts, mobility patterns, archival discoveries, and development interests underlying urban planning schemes and city-building initiatives. Ms. Music has been featured in documentaries on HBO, PBS, Peacock, Amazon Prime, and the History Channel, and has performed one-woman shows and poetry on stages including the Detroit Symphony and Detroit Opera.

My late father, Joe Von Battle, is believed to be the first Black, post-World War II independent record producer in the United States. He opened up a record store in Detroit in 1945, which serviced a vibrant community called Black Bottom for its dark soil—a largely segregated community where Black residents who migrated from Southern states resided from the twenties to fifties. Born in 1954, the eldest of four children with his second wife, I spent much time around record shops in my early years, immersed in music. In my teens, the 1967 Rebellion was precipitated by a police raid of an unlicensed, after-hours social club, and was one of the bloodiest urban riots recorded in American history. In its aftermath, steeped in the social turmoil of the time, I became a student activist and, in my twenties, a labor union president, followed by 30 years with the county courts, until my retirement. Through it all, I have been a writer and a witness.

Fig. 1: Marsha Music in the doorway of her father's record shop on Hastings Street, 1960

My father made a recording studio in the back of his shop, producing folks from the vibrant community on old Hastings Street. He recorded mostly Blues and Gospel and is notable for producing the first gospel records of internationally renowned music artist, and undisputed Queen of Soul, Aretha Franklin. My parents moved, when I was a toddler, from Detroit to Highland Park—a separate city within the city of Detroit—a tiny, lush, green municipality. Highland Park was the home of Ford Motor Company's first assembly line factory, and I grew up in the last years of the city's overflowing prosperity. This was sustained by a tax base subsidized by Ford, Chrysler Corporation and more, and I attended some of the best public schools in America. After World War II, as whites began leaving Detroit and Highland Park, the city became a centrifugal force in the development of a Black middle class in this country.

An autodidact, I write and speak about Detroit's post-midcentury existence as a Black city. Yet I explore our multinational and multiracial origins as an underpinning force of the past, conundrum of the present and guidepost to the future. In 2013, I performed my first one-woman show, Marsha Music—Live From Hastings Street, in which I tell the story of my family and its intersection with the history of Detroit. I have performed this multimedia show on many stages in Detroit. My work has focused on place-based narratives pertaining to Detroit neighborhoods. An audacious line from my show and writings that has resonance for both myself and audiences is: "Some people say that they have come to save Detroit, but I say, they have come to Detroit to be saved."

① Black Bottom was "the most culturally significant community in [the state of] Michigan," says Jamon Jordan, Detroit's Official Historian. It was the heart of immigration for people from many parts of the world in the early last century. As those immigrants moved out and were allowed to become "white," it became majority Black, and was the place to which numbers of Black people were effectively segregated after their migration from the South. My father's record shop was a few miles away from our Highland Park home, just outside Black Bottom, and, in the fifties, the community was destroyed in the name of urban renewal. A decade later, my father was forced to move his Hastings Street business to make way for the I-375 Chrysler freeway. He moved to the Twelfth Street community across town, but things were different. A mere seven years later, police brutality and the upheaval of the time resulted in the Detroit Rebellion of 1967, where my father, and many others, lost everything. To add to this turmoil, I was with child in high school, left before graduating and moved a few miles away, to Detroit. Despondent in the midst of his troubles, my father was consumed with alcoholism until he died in 1973.

30 years later, after living in several neighborhoods in Detroit, I returned to live in the family home in Highland Park and experienced the city's heartbreaking diminution, due to its abandonment by Ford, Chrysler, et al. Amid the social devastation that followed, I witnessed the community's determination to maintain pride and possession of their extraordinary homes and community. I began writing about my father's life and times, and I was there several years before losing the house in an electrical fire in 2007. After regrouping, I returned to Detroit, a single mother with two sons, and moved near downtown to Lafayette Park, to the community designed by German designer Mies van der Rohe and built on vacant land that once was Black Bottom. I grew up in a vortex of change.

In 1805, Detroit experienced the ultimate catastrophic change—the entire city, then about six hundred residents, burned to the ground, due to a barn fire that spread uncontrollably. From this calamity came one of the city's mottos, "Speramus Meliora; Resurget Cineribus," meaning "We hope for better things; It will rise from the ashes," a clarion call for rebirth. Roughly 150 years later, catastrophe struck the city once again, this time in the form of the 1967 uprising, popularly known as The Rebellion, at the time the largest disturbance of its kind in American history. The rage on display during The Rebellion was primarily directed towards the rabid police brutality that permeated the community, as well as discriminatory roadblocks to access and opportunities in housing, workplaces, and education. In addition, the Twelfth Street community, the epicenter of the conflagration, was populated by thousands who had been expelled from Black Bottom and Hastings Street, less than a decade before, which was an underlying cause of wrath for many. Their new homes and apartments in the Twelfth Street community were the substantial brick behemoths of the West Side, but they were trapped in the confines of homes often packed with multiple families, on blocks teeming with those unable to move to wherever else their money might allow them to afford. The destruction resulted in the eventual widening of a section of Twelfth Street into the two-way, center-median boulevard that we see today.

In the aftermath of The Rebellion of 1967, the exodus of whites from the city, which had begun in the forties, continued in earnest, and Detroit became majority Black. But we can also trace a different kind of shift to this period, one no less seismic than the great Detroit fire and the events of

"As I am wont to say, whites did not merely flee—*white flight*, as it is known—but were often driven out of the city by real estate developers and homeowner's associations using *racial fears* to entice them from their homes."

1967. This was a shift in narrative—placing responsibility for Detroit's destruction on its Black residents, despite their efforts, in the face of economic decline and industrial desertion, to uplift themselves and to maintain and restore what remained of their communities. Evidence of ruin was visible, but evidence of what had been salvaged by Black Detroiters residing in otherwise intact neighborhoods was invisible. It is this invisibility that defines recent depictions of Detroit's Black residents, the roots of which are explored in the history—both personal and collective—unraveled in this piece.

By the turn of the twentieth century, Detroit was one of the richest cities in the world, even before the introduction of the automobile. With the growth of industrialization and commerce, Detroit exploded with exceptional wealth—ironworks for the manufacturing of stoves, tools and implements, and the production of cigars, carbon coal, and top hats—made possible by the extermination of the buffalo. Indigenous peoples' fur trapping and sales were appropriated, as well as their crops, forestry, and lifestyle, by alliances, trickery, skirmishes, and wars. Owners, architects, and builders used much of this wealth to emulate the great houses of Europe, developing grand, Gilded Age mansions comparable to the grand mansions of New York.

We baby-boomer schoolchildren were taught, "Detroit is the Paris of the West," an axiom that had emerged a century earlier for a city that had become renowned for its opulence. The commercial and residential architecture and street design, emanating in spokes from downtown, were inspired by and evoked the French metropolis. Visitors at the turn of the century were enthralled when they arrived in our city, setting their watches and clocks to the central timepiece of old City Hall—the largest clock in the United States. Later, art deco structures such as the Fisher and Guardian Buildings became revered as singular architectural masterpieces. It was a place of jaw-dropping grandeur. Mansions and castles dotted streets that had to be widened to accommodate the upsurge in population and traffic—first horses, then automobiles. The city teemed with the noise and dust of construction. By the late nineteenth century, many significant structures were being demolished due to an obsession with "the new." With the advent of the automobile, and the development of homes and neighborhoods fit for the moguls of the new era, Detroit's wealth grew exponentially. Stunning new buildings were so ubiquitous on the urban landscape that they became ordinary, in part because they were repurposed for utilitarian uses.

Contrary to belief, Black Detroiters have always been accustomed to navigating outstanding architecture, even while carrying out mundane daily tasks such as bill paying and physician visits. In Detroit neighborhoods, the architectural distinction of the homes and buildings with which we live remains evident, regardless of their condition. Post-World War II, the first wave of whites began to be manipulated out of the city by the racialized fearmongering of real estate interests anxious to develop the suburbs to which industry had fled. Federal government policies, such as the G.I. Bill, and financing via the Federal Housing Administration, supported building and buying in the suburbs, not the city. These forces began developing areas across the Eight Mile boundary of Detroit, as whites rushed out in response to the instigated panic. As I am wont to say, whites did not merely flee—white flight, as it is known— but were often driven out of the city by real estate developers and homeowner's associations using racial fears to entice them from their homes. This was a phenomenon generally of the early post-World War II years; the later, post-sixties exodus was due to numerous factors, such as crime, which was inevitable in a city financially collapsing and penetrated by the drug trade, and an education system in disarray from the population drain. By the mid-sixties, many middle-class Black people were also moving for these reasons. Later, there was a removal of residency requirements, allowing police and firefighters to live outside of the city's borders.

As white people left, monied Black professionals moved out of historically segregated neighborhoods such as Black Bottom, where they had resided since the early twentieth century. Although Black Bottom had lovely Victorian homes and buildings, the grand homes of the city were not occupied by Black people in the early last century. By the mid-forties, the backbone of segregation was breaking through legal and social reforms, and even before our ascendency to early-to-late sixties musical dominance and political power, we began to move into architecturally rich places such as Brush Park, Uptown, Boston-Edison and Arden Park. Ironically, many who had fled the Jim Crow restrictions under the shadow of formidable Southern plantation houses, came to be the owners of similarly grand, pillared houses in Detroit. Later, well-to-do communities such as Indian Village, Palmer Woods, Sherwood Forest, Rosedale Park, etc., included not just Black professionals and civic leaders but the upper strata of the industrial working class, with an unparalleled blue-collar affluence befitting the highest-paid proletarians in the world. In these neighborhoods are homes of incomparable stateliness, and this majestic built environment contributed to the indomitable persona of Black Detroiters, and our sense of personal power and worth.

Of the many profound changes that Detroiters have experienced, few are more significant than this demographic shift, both in terms of geography and population. Despite contributing to Detroit's ascendancy as a Black majority city and playing an integral role in shaping the city's culture and built environment, Black people themselves have been decoupled from narratives pertaining to the city's architecture and economic power. This is especially egregious because Black people not only came to own these beautiful homes, but their vision and labor were essential to the continuation of the broader urban landscape left behind. Yet, somehow, as the city's Black population grew, there was a notable absence of images of Detroit's opulent housing stock in films, news and architectural media, evidence of a de facto campaign to ignore the grand environs in which thousands of Black Detroiters lived—and lived well. Many outsiders, who often only know the city via social media and Google maps, erroneously believe that the more sumptuous neighborhoods must be mostly white. Instead of respectfully recognizing their existence, urban narratives and representations of Detroit have often either erased Black people or depicted them as living in ruination with little to no economic, cultural, or social power.

To understand Black peoples' mainstream invisibility within their own magnificent, Black majority city, one must delve into the reality of the belief that it is impossible for us to own and maintain beautiful real estate. Suburban visitors to estate sales, home tours and such are often agog at the opulence in which many Black Detroiters have obviously been living, particularly when all of their lives they have been told that Detroit is a hellhole. At a moving sale for a 15,000 square-foot mansion, I witnessed stunned customers addressing a Black woman in the house as if she were "the help," and her unruffled reply that she was, in fact, the homeowner.

Filmmakers prefer to capture images of destruction, rather than the even more remarkable phenomenon of the architectural abundance in which many of us have lived for decades. This erasure also serves to obscure the incongruity—and irrationality—of the wholesale abandonment of these remarkable properties for the suburbs. Chroniclers of the history of these architecturally significant homes often recount their original white architects and provenance, omit the decades-long midcentury Black residency, and skip forward to champion the new white owners and residents of today—a maddening, compartmentalized history. Some Black residents prefer to stay under the radar, lest attention be drawn and efforts made to separate them from their spectacular properties, a phenomenon for which there is historical precedent in this country.

Despite the plethora of images of bedraggled homes and buildings in disrepair, houses with intricate stained-glass windows, ornamental metal and staircases, decorative wood and tile work, and other intact embellishments belie narratives of neglect and deterioration, affirming the reality of decades of devoted maintenance and care. Detroiters are condemned for the degradation of the city—whether openly stated or implied—yet our role in preserving what remains oft goes unnoted. Detroit is a city with a distinct irony, the relative prosperity engendered by the auto industry and ancillary capital created an unprecedented Black affluence. Unlike in some major cities, where segregation could be maintained by economic inequality, countless Black residents actually could afford to live wherever they wanted and this had to be stopped. A principal means of accomplishing this was via restrictive covenants in real estate deeds, preventing sales to Black people, and creating narratives wherein Black homeowners were regarded as less capable of sumptuous, orderly living. The idea that a people, with ancestors who had once been enslaved, could live in these architectural wonders was intolerable. There were few glowing features in architectural media, nationally or locally, normally befitting of a place with such significant housing stock. Yet, since the middle of the last century, generations of Black families have been nurtured and raised in architectural wonders. Most substantive neighborhoods, even the most sumptuous, are majority Black. Which is

Fig. 2: Marsha Music on the service drive of the freeway that replaced old Hastings Street

a surprise to many, although a few have become or are becoming largely white—for gentrification is real.

② I speak to young people regarding the causes of the devastation of their neighborhoods, and the defeat, shame, and mistaken notion that this was a community suffering a self-inflicted wound.

In the book Detroit City Is the Place to Be, Mark Binelli wrote about the day I entered a meeting of newcomers and others and challenged the excessive promotion of images of ruin with which we native Detroiters had to live. Yet some of my most beloved artist friends create in the milieu of devastation, transforming land, abandoned houses and forsaken urban dross into ornamented dreamscapes and odes to survival and loss. There needs to be more attention paid to the splendor of the built environment that has survived—the luscious greenspaces created by residents. Tours of homes, gardens and backyard ponds reveal environs of amazing aesthetics, worthy of the same international exposure as the city's supposed ruination. I wrote a poem, The Doll House, about our amazing homes in Detroit, that in 2024 was displayed as a visual arts installation at Detroit Contemporary Gallery.

"We will rise from the ashes." Again, in Detroit, this axiom, a clarion call for rebirth, came into play. The devastation of the Twelfth Street community during the 1967 uprising was a turning point in the visual imagery of the city, with the proliferation of images of ruin. Yet contrary to popular belief, most of the city was untouched by the destruction. It was not the aftermath of 1967, but the tsunami of the eighties' foreclosure crisis and beyond, that brought the most widespread destruction of properties, especially residential. Much of this destruction was due to the deliberate burning of innumerable structures, with some fires rumored to have been set by owners of Detroit properties outside of the city, seeking to cash in on the fiasco of underwater mortgages. In this crisis, entire blocks of homes were destroyed and whole neighborhoods erased, often in less than a decade. This wave of devastation resulted in images that ranged from desolate to macabre, captured by photographers worldwide and so ubiquitous as to be

Fig. 3:
Joe Von Battle in front of his record shop on Hastings Street, Detroit, circa 1956

Fig. 4: Marsha Music at Michigan Central, during the last days before the start of restoration, 2018

dubbed "ruin porn." Once more, "Speramus Meliora; Resurget Cineribus" became the adage of the times.

More recently, a form of looting has taken its toll on the city's architectural landscape. The scrapping of houses for their construction elements and ornamental details, a significant amount of which found its way into homes and structures in suburbia, out of state and, improbably, out of the country. Pundits decry poor and working-class scrappers stealing elements and ornamentation from historic places yet turn a blind eye to the upscale market for Detroit's treasures. Many, out of necessity, restore Detroit homes with elements originally ransacked from the decimated built environment. With this mining of Detroit's supply of extraordinary stained and leaded glass, wood paneling and floors, decorative features, etc., the half has never been told regarding this wholesale plundering. In fact, the recent restoration of the Michigan Central Station was accompanied by a call for the return—sans punishment or accountability—of elements that had found their way to places far, far from Detroit. Many items, some massive, had been removed and housed in locations, discrete or otherwise, during the years of abandonment, with officials deftly avoiding the word "stolen."

The ruination and visual devastation, predominant in media, resulted in generations of Detroiters defined by relentless views of destruction and decay. The amount of empty land in the city is shocking when first seen by visitors; it is even shocking to us at times. I proffer that our children who are immersed in communities of ruination grow up with what I call "retinal scars," impacting all areas of life and psyche. Predictably, as newcomers moved into the city, many who relished this destruction as gritty and cool now cry out against how their city is portrayed. After years of enduring such fare, it is evidently now unacceptable that the city's new residents live in a city besmirched by such imagery, compromising their property values.

3   In my essay The Kidnapped Children of Detroit, I chronicled my first-person view of the post-World War II so-called white flight. Those "kidnapped children" being the boomer-era kids snatched from their increasingly Black neighborhoods—and friends—by their fearful parents. In this work, I contemplate the movement and impact of those who have returned to the city of their parents and grandparents who left generations ago. In 2015, I wrote what has become my signature, epic poem, Just Say Hi—The Gentrification Blues, my admonishment to newcomers who ignore the customs of Black Detroiters in whose communities they now live—especially the practice of speaking or saying "Hi." Such lapses in social mores are a form of the invisibility that characterizes social dynamics between Black and white. My poems and essays highlight elements of Detroit life oft ignored by media and city pundits. As an observer and unraveller of problematic social dynamics, it is tricky traversing these issues. In this poem I suggested saying "Hi" as a simple starting point of

JUST SAY HI

All around Detroit we talk, from shops to congregations
There's much discussion of the city's new Gentrification
and all the changes with the folks a'moving to the D
the changes in our lifetime thought we'd never live to see
We talk about The Newcomers, with righteous consternation,
ol' school exasperation, 'bout a disconcerting thing –
"They don't even SPEAK!" we say, when we get on the subject
our mantra of rejection of invisibility..........Just Say Hi

respect and engagement. In 2018 I read it at Detroit Homecoming, a dynamic annual event welcoming Detroit expats to the city and engaging their support, and have read it at many events before and since.

Speaking of words, there is a common refrain, "Detroit is coming back!" Yet this seemingly positive, upbeat expression actually turns reality on its head. It is a swift, semantic elimination of reality, especially ironic when coming from suburbanites and expats. For at the root of its decline, Detroit did not leave; Detroit was left. This phrase bespeaks the tension of differing relationships to the city, the micro-erasures inherent in the most seemingly innocuous of statements, that mask difficult truths. When confronted with this upside-down adage—"Detroit is coming back!"—many Detroiters now respond with "Detroit never left!" Some even add "You did!" Today, the revival of interest and development in the city is at a fever pitch. The midcentury focus on populating the suburbs, in order to support the industries and infrastructure that had abandoned Detroit, has shifted to the redevelopment of Detroit properties that many monied owners had left to rot. Developers boomerang back to areas that they or their forebears helped devalue generations before, now that they are potentially profitable. Even institutions of higher learning return, after decades departed. Developers new to the game jump in the development fray.

The Detroiters of the late last century came to maturity in an atmosphere of vitriol and contempt, directed at the city and its residents. The animus hurled at Black Detroiters, by those often removed generations from the city, was prominent in the atmosphere. Living in a devalued and maligned city, called a "hellhole" and "Detoilet" by toxic jokesters, it is no surprise that, for many Detroiters, a sense of pride in the environment was real but challenging, for it takes much to transcend such hatred. In the eighties, city booster Emily Gail began a campaign, popularizing "Say nice things about Detroit," a seemingly innocuous slogan that was, in reality, a courageous response to the derision directed at the city. A town once renowned as the pinnacle of good living became the target of venom as the city became increasingly Black.

Yet, neighborhoods and homes of great provenance and even majesty remained. Growing up, as I did, in the midst of architectural glory—Arts and Crafts bungalows and mini-mansions—I realize that it had a profound effect on the way that my peers and I saw ourselves, though we had little historical knowledge of our surroundings. We witnessed the wholesale rejection of these homes for the suburbs by our white neighbors, caught in the fever of being driven across Eight Mile. Perhaps we absorbed the devaluation implicit in their leaving, a kind of community gaslighting—for what value could our homes possibly have, jettisoned, as they were, like used tissues as our neighbors ran? But many of our Black elders knew, opining wryly, that there was more than a little something to the solid, sumptuous spaces in which we lived. They looked on in amusement and disdain at those lured to the new homes in suburbia, which our elders regarded as inferior to our solid brick homes. Many senior Detroiters knew the day would come that there would be a return, and with it, an appreciation of the value of the homes that were left behind.

Many stories and images, or lack thereof, have influenced the view of Detroit nationally and internationally. One such characterization is the absence of Black people in many visual or written narratives—incongruous in a city that is still majority Black. It is common to see historic images of the last century that include no

Black people, despite our exponentially growing presence after the nineteen-twenties. Renderings of contemporary construction projects have depicted only whites populating new spaces—conceivably imagining life without Black people—to the outrage of the community. There are neighborhoods that are not only intact, but glorious—maintained by a majority Black population that held on during years of the city's effective embargo. The Historical Detroit Area Architecture and Historic Homes of Detroit groups on Facebook have done much to expose the architecture of the city to an international audience. However, in the public imagination and media, there is often a tendency to separate the long-time Black residents from these communities, with the implication that it is the return of whites that has midwifed the beauty of these homes.

Additionally, beneath the shining new city is a heaving dragon, roiling discontentedly beneath the new pavement. Much of Detroit is scarred by the ruin for which the city has been known. After years of economic decline, in an unprecedented action, the city declared bankruptcy and was subsequently led by an unelected emergency management. Public services, though improved after the reorganization, are still wanting in areas, and activists maintain that funds for services are siphoned into Downtown.

> "Communities seeking to attain property are *pitted against land grabs* by monied forces."

Residents, who cannot get community ventures off the ground, look dubiously at projects in their midst, granted millions. Despite new housing in neighborhoods, many residents are hopeful yet flinch at the appearance of white developers on their blocks planning more projects which neither they nor their children can afford. Black developers have a presence too, with projects ostensibly less problematic.

The Michigan Department of Transportation has embarked upon the reconfiguration of the I-375 Freeway that ended Hastings Street; the plans have the community up in arms. There is hope for the new and a seething too. After decades of vitriolic disparagement of the city and its majority Black population, city leaders, developers and concerns of public relations have the Herculean task of shifting public impressions of the city in the opposite direction. Civic boosters are faced with a conundrum: how to reverse decades of pernicious, anti-Detroit narratives that permeated the atmosphere, serving the needs of prior generations of suburban developers. Today, they sing the opposite tune to silence the drumbeat of toxic anti-Detroitism and promote a city that is suddenly the greatest place in the world—a whole new song.

My calling is to observe and articulate conflicting impulses dominating discourse in Detroit, to address the disparagement of the city while acknowledging its pitfalls, and to recognize the reality of gentrification and also the need for development. For they are not synonymous, there could be development without displacement—if there is the will. The changes here are dizzying, with new explorations and projects emerging daily, yet accompanied by an underpinning of internecine political, financial, and artistic warring beneath the surface. The atmosphere is intense—for all of the arts events, urban gardens and openings, there are evictions, skyrocketing rents, displacements. That said, the energy in the Detroit arts community has been likened to the Harlem Renaissance, what with the intensity all over the city.

DETROIT—INVISIBILITY IN THE MAGNIFICENT CITY

4   I am honored to be noted as a co-producer of a documentary film, This Is Detroit, now in post-production, which explores efforts of Detroiters, from urban gardeners to thought leaders. I was part of a multimedia project called Land, a documentary film and theatrical project exploring the past and present Belgian community in Detroit, presented in Europe. In a documentary film, Detroit, Comeback City, I attempted to paint a picture of my family's arrival in Detroit, via Michigan Central Train Depot—now known as Michigan Central, sans trains—and in a documentary series project produced by the late Anthony Bourdain—his last project before his tragic passing, yet to be released—I was extensively interviewed, and talked about my family's Michigan Central origins in Detroit.

If not for Michigan Central, I might not be in Detroit today. My father arrived in 1937 from Macon, Georgia, escaping the Jim Crow South, living with his older brother until he could bring his wife and children here to join him—I, the eldest of his second family, was not yet thought of. When they arrived to meet him at the Michigan Central Train Depot and disembarked, he embraced them in jubilation, with the towering frontage of the station in the background. Even in their eighties, recounting this, my older half-siblings' remembrances of those moments at the station were as crystalline as the day they occurred.

In many respects, the changes in Detroit are nothing short of miraculous; areas of the city are again bursting with volcanic eruptions of the "new." The Detroit Riverfront, once a rocky stretch of old industrial and warehouse buildings—and cool, old bars—is now a stunning waterfront walkway, regarded as the best riverfront in the United States, despite recent allegations of financial wrongdoings by the CEO. Downtown, once grim, and sparsely populated—except for the businesses, Black artists and entrepreneurs who remained there—is unrecognizable to returning visitors; the change has been so remarkable, and there are many areas of redevelopment outside of Downtown. The recent NFL draft, the talent-selecting event of the National Football League, was a tsunami of sports-loving humanity that converged upon a Downtown dressed up for the occasion. But more than a story about football, and the expenditures of millions of NFL dollars in a financially challenged city, it was a signaling of another point on a trajectory of change: with over 750,000 gathered Downtown, there was a new, diverse level of engagement between visitors and Detroiters, one that proceeded without incident.

On June 6, 2024, Detroit celebrated the long-awaited reopening of the iconic Michigan Central, also known as The Train Station—although with no trains for the time being. Built in 1913, this landmark reopened after decades of abandonment, neglect, and in more recent years of intensive restoration, the most significant transformation of the architectural landscape to date. The abandoned train station was a powerful, visual metaphor for the decimation of Detroit. Its colossal presence was the epitome of ruination, a reminder of the city's former greatness, a harbinger of its unrelenting decline. Owned by a developer that allowed it to continue to decay, it was bought in recent years by the Ford Motor Company. Bill Ford, grandson of Henry Ford I, envisioned the resurrection of the site. His spearheading of the project, and the raising of nearly one billion dollars from private and public coffers to make it a reality, is a reckoning with his predecessor's leaving of Detroit—an atonement for the past, if you will. It is a spectacular gesture, this center of Ford's new mobility

Fig. 5: Marsha Music at Roosevelt Park, during the celebration of its restoration and reopening, Michigan Central in background

Fig. 6: Marsha Music's book, the Detroitist

technology. It is a look to the future, the ultimate redevelopment of the devalued.

In its evocation of the memories of bygone Detroit, Michigan Central is a place of nostalgia, a longing for the good old days, both real and imaginary. Many, including me, burst into tears upon entering the grand edifice. Many whites, disconnected from the city for decades, grieved not only for their old lives and times in Detroit, but for the city itself, and many Black visitors shed the same tears as they entered the station's magnificent portals. But some say that Michigan Central and its branding is a symbol of the return of whites to Detroit, and for the thousands who arrived for the opening, this was indeed a great coming home. Conscious of it or not, many mourn the times before the Black majority in Detroit—evoked in much of the imagery of the station's grand corridors—despite, in real life, the ubiquitous presence of Black people at the train station since its construction. Such invisibility of our presence, in memory and time, is the very embodiment of the contradictions inherent in such a momentous change. Black people too have many memories of Michigan Central. Pullman porters—legendary attendants in the cars, and early leaders of the labor movement—navigated difficult social and racial interactions. They carried

> "Detroit does not have a Black community, as in other major cities; it is *a Black city in which others also live.*"

clandestine news and information about the Civil Rights Movement in the South and the living conditions for Black people in the North—an overground railroad, so to speak. Some elders remember how, in the South, traveling to Detroit, they boarded the Jim Crow cars. Once they crossed the infamous Mason-Dixon line, they disembarked from the segregated cars and re-entered the cars in the front. The process was reversed on their return. Michigan Central Train Depot was the unforgettable point of origin for thousands of us arriving in Detroit from the South, seeking new lives and opportunities. It is important that our presence in history be accurately reflected in the nostalgia and imagery surrounding the revitalized Michigan Central.

The opening days of Michigan Central were an ecstatic celebration marking the resurrection of not only the building, but the city itself. The opening concert was a spectacular event, with big stars like Eminem, Diana Ross, Jack White, and Fantasia. Later concert events during the opening summer featured great local artists, embedded in the community. It must also be said that many white newcomers look dubiously at the transformation of Michigan Central, for some came intentionally to a Detroit that they experienced as a rough and gritty playground, preferring that it stay that way. They often do not grasp that the lavishness of the newly resurrected Michigan Central was a reality of Detroiters' lives; it is the decay that is the anomaly. Some such critics have resisted renovation and luxury development as being too lavish for Detroiters, with some of the basic needs of the community unmet, but this is often just contempt and condescension masquerading as social consciousness. For Detroit is a city that was once the very pinnacle of high life and style, where even the poor could live in stately homes, dressed and coiffed to the proverbial nines. For long-time local Black Detroiters, the opulence of Michigan Central is a return to the grandeur to which we were accustomed. One would hope that the largesse of Ford or some other entity could be extended to the restoration of the abandoned Ford assembly plant in Highland Park, which Ford no longer owns; representing a full-circle transformation made whole.

5 The question is: Invisible to who? To the "white gaze," as author Toni Morrison says? As in Ralph Ellison's book Invisible Man, about Black invisibility? Clearly, we have not been invisible to one another, knowing full well the reality of our existence. But I, like many other Black people, have experienced being invisible to whites—literally unseen. So, it is not a stretch to imagine that entire communities can experience the same phenomenon. Here, in this new Detroit, we resist this invisibility.

Many Black Detroiters believe that we will be pushed out of the city, that the plan is to make it white again—a not unjustified suspicion. Slowly, the percentage of Black citizens has dipped lower, now 77.7 percent. Many find it difficult, if not impossible, to find housing that is actually affordable in the city, as opposed to affordable by the standards of developers. Some have been pushed out into less pricey suburbs—a generational bait and switch, after promises of a better life in Detroit, decades ago.

But the Blackness of Detroit is the very soul of the city. We assert our presence in new spaces that many thought to be off-limits in the new Detroit. Michigan Central's community leadership includes a cohort of Black excellence. Black entrepreneurs persevere in the ownership of new businesses. Hundreds of tech-savvy folks congregate at Black Tech Saturdays at New Lab, part of the Michigan Central campus, and white photographer Stephen McGee created massive portraits of Black Detroiters, including me, that were placed in and outside of Michigan Central during its opening festivities—in an intentional effort to counter invisibility. Black Detroiter Tiff Massey is the youngest artist to ever have a solo exhibit at the Detroit Institute of Arts, with a groundbreaking installation called Seven Mile and Livernois, named after a juncture of two streets of dynamic post-midcentury Black life in Detroit. The new Shepherd Arts Center campus features a towering outdoor installation of the work of the late Black Detroit artist Charles McGee, and houses residency spaces of Modern Ancient Brown, founded by McArthur Binion, for BIPOC arts scholars. The Detroit Fine Arts Breakfast Club, a lively, diverse gathering of artists, meets weekly. The city vibrates with innumerable arts events and activities, reminiscent of the Harlem Renaissance.

Although the changes in Detroit have been attributed to the current—white—Mayor, Mike Duggan, elected twice in the Black city, these seismic shifts emanate from powers and the movement of capital well beyond the influence of a single individual. Detroit experienced Black social and political power writ large in the late last century, and regardless of the color of the city's current leader, Black experience, ingenuity, wisdom, and connections oscillate beneath the surface of all endeavors, where the dynamism of our history and existence asserts itself. The skills honed by generations of trade unionism, civil rights activism, and social and civic leadership still manifest, disrupting narratives of invisibility. The task remains to attract more of the Black middle class back to the city, and to shore up the lives and housing of the community that has held on through the worst of times.

The color pendulum is swinging, but what is needed is increased recognition of the decades of perseverance, vigilance and labor that has preserved much in these communities. A new, winding walkway named the Joe Louis Greenway, after the legendary Detroit boxer, is being carved out of old railway lines. The path meanders in a horseshoe shape, stretching from the riverfront and looping back through "the hood"—areas that have seen little to no development in the last hundred years. A transformation indeed that will doubtlessly bring with it new residents to old neighborhoods. The changes in Detroit reveal our unfinished business, and despite errors and entitlements that plague our relations, many newcomers break generational curses and learn to live among us. Detroit does not have a Black community, as in other major cities; it is a Black city in which others also live. We are here, as newcomers arrive to this magnificent, green city and we are not invisible.

The events described herein only touch the surface of the maelstrom of change in Detroit. In 2015, representatives from UNESCO arrived from Graz, Austria, to meet with civic and institutional leaders, and ultimately named Detroit as a UNESCO City of Design—the first and only city so chosen in the United States, and a recognition of the city's aesthetic greatness, including our built environment. My ancillary discussions with them were a factor in their determination.

The coronavirus pandemic hit Detroit particularly hard, with a tragic number of deaths. I was deeply troubled by this catastrophic assault on the community and began writing about it in 2020 during the lockdown. Confined to my home, I was interviewed on Zoom and from the park outside, by news outlets such as MSNBC, and was featured in the Los Angeles Times for my work articulating the profound losses of this debacle. In the midst of the pandemic, I was commissioned by Yuval Sharon, Creative Director of Detroit Opera, to write the narration for Twilight Gods, a new version of the Wagnerian opera. It was performed in the opera house's multi-story parking garage during the pandemic and received critical acclaim. It was a balm to many during that chapter of international loss. I have experienced my own losses, including the passing of my husband, internationally acclaimed artist David Philpot, before the pandemic, and the loss of my eldest son in a motorcycle accident during this writing.

I continue to integrate urban planning, place-based policies, and intangible cultural heritage—local narratives, daily rituals, and sacred spaces—into narratives that provide deeply intimate insider perspectives and structural and spatial analyses of Detroit. I am coproducing a documentary with film-maker Juanita Anderson on my father's life and times—Hastings Street Blues. I am honored to be called a Detroit cultural luminary and unofficial ambassador. In 2019, I published my inaugural book, The Detroitist, and I am featured in the internationally acclaimed Advanced Style fashion series, in books and on social media. I have completed writing the narration for a riverfront project, Core I-375, produced by artist Michelle Andonian, a multi-disciplinary exploration of the layers of history beneath and beyond the I-375 and Chrysler Freeway that replaced old Hastings Street. In 2023, I received the Spirit of Detroit Award, a Special Tribute from the State of Michigan, and was nominated for a National Endowment of the Arts. I am on the Board of Directors of the Detroit Institute of Arts and am active in my community. It is an exciting time and place to live, where I preach the gospel of Detroit.

THANKS TO THE HISTORY KEEPERS

Jamon Jordan Official Historian of the City of Detroit/tours
Ken Coleman historian/tours
Dan Austin Michigan Central and historicdetroit.org
Juanita Anderson filmmaker, head of Media Arts and Study, Wayne State University
Marcia Black and Alexis Garcia, Emily Kutil Black Bottom Archives/ Black Bottom Streetview
Joe Von Battle Jr. and my other siblings, who keep our memories alive
Olayami Dabls MBAD Bead Museum, African/Detroit cultural intersection
Gregory Fornier author, Detroit history stories
Tim Kiska journalist, Detroit History Podcast
William Frank founder, Historic Homes of Detroit, on Facebook

Ben Gravel founder, Historical Detroit Area Architecture, on Facebook
Michelle Mckinney President, Detroit Sound Conservancy
Carleton Gholz founder, Detroit Sound Conservancy
Carlos Nielbock architectural ornamental metal artist / YouTube
Rod Arroyo historical researcher, midcentury Black business
Gregory J. Reed attorney, archivist, producer
Karen Risko, Jeanette Pierce, Linda Yellen tours, general Detroit history
Adam Stanfel, Tino Gross, Michael Hurtt Detroit music history
Sharon Sexton filmmaker, author, historical reenactor
Jiam Desjardins, Bert Dearing esteemed citizen historians; Black Bottom, Hastings, etc.

A conversation between   Lukáš Berberich   & Karl Stocker

Film Can Say
Everything At Once

LUKÁŠ BERBERICH is a film and music producer and programmer. He is the director of Kino Úsmev, an art house cinema in Košice, Slovakia, which he has co-founded and directed since 2015. He is a founding member of the Cinefil association and from 2002 to 2005, he worked as cinema programmer at the Cinefil film club in Košice. He was the music programmer for, among others, Vice magazine in Prague and for Tabačka Kulturfabrik in Košice. He co-founded the independent music label Exitab. He was the artistic director for Moonride and Poke festivals. As a producer and cultural manager, he worked on a number of international film, music, theatre and visual art projects, such as the performance project X-Apartments, the international cooperation of cultural centres Engine Room Europe, the international music project Phuterdo Øre, and many others. He participated in fora for audiovisual arts professionals at festivals in New York, Tokyo, Berlin, San Sebastian and Venice.

K S What led you down this path in life, working to develop Košice in different creative fields?

L B As a teenager and young punk roaming the streets of Košice, I got hooked on art. It started as a passion for visual arts; I was obsessed with becoming a sculptor. Then I stumbled upon Dostoevsky's idea that the world would be saved by beauty, and it hit me hard. I still believe in that. Later, I discovered film and it blew my mind how it fuses all forms of art into one powerful medium. Film became my new obsession—raw, complex, and able to say everything at once.

K S Can you describe some concrete projects which you have done in Košice and why do you like them?

L B I have had the chance to work on a lot of international artistic projects. It is hard to choose just a few, as there are so many. As a producer though, I particularly enjoy projects that I am involved with from the very beginning, where we create an idea that excites us so much, we simply have to find the resources to make it happen.

One of those is Angrusori. It has got nothing to do with film, but it is an exciting collaboration between traditional Roma musicians from eastern Slovakia and experimental musicians from Norway. Together, we created this fusion of experimental jazz, world music, and Roma songs. It is a large ensemble, but we have managed to record and release an award-winning album in the United Kingdom and have been touring internationally.

Another project I loved being part of is X-Apartments; an original theater format by the German director Matthias Lilienthal. It is a series of short performances in private spaces, like regular people's apartments, with a different artist for each show.

Fig. 1: Kino Úsmev in the fall of 2015

We managed to get artists from around the world—Lebanon, Australia, Germany, the UK, Poland and Austria. The audience toured these apartments in pairs, making it super intimate and powerful.

And then, there is our inclusive cinema work. This is something I am really proud of. We have been breaking new ground by making cinemas accessible to people with various disadvantages that might otherwise prevent them from visiting a typical movie screening in the first place, like people with a vision or hearing impairment, autism or, because of recent events, kids from Ukraine. We have been pushing this nationally, and our team even runs workshops and offers consultancy internationally. We also run the annual Inclusive Film Festival, which is not just a safe space for the audience, it is a breeding ground for new ideas on how to make the cinema attractive to everyone.

K S How have your activities in film, festivals, and the arts, especially your work at Kino Úsmev, shaped people's lives?

L B I think our work packs a punch and hopefully adds a small piece to the bigger picture of change. I have learned that it is not just about what you do, but how you do it that makes a true impact. Our work is not just about showing great films, it is about making sure our values, like inclusivity, openness, and connecting different people, shine through. Kino Úsmev is not just a cinema; it is a space where we smash through barriers and get people talking.

K S How does this connect with political and social change?

L B Somehow, our space has turned into a hotspot for politicians to make appearances. While the aim is not to get political, the fact that they show up means they recognize the power of what we are doing—although they are less inclined to back us financially. I hope what we do can shake things up in the community and spark some positive change. When we started this project, we had just returned from abroad, pouring our time and money into something we believed Košice needed. We had big dreams, and I still believe we can do more. But seeing the current political mess in Slovakia, it is clear we have a lot more work ahead of us.

K S What have been the reactions to your work?

L B It is definitely not all sunshine and rainbows. We have taken some heavy hits from people who do not align with our values—whether it is inclusivity, anti-racism, or fighting xenophobia. Social media can be brutal, and it is tough on my colleagues who are working tirelessly and busting their asses for little pay—cultural work in Slovakia does not exactly pay the bills. But we also receive a lot of positive feedback, and that keeps us going. We are gaining international recognition, but we always stay grounded and remain attuned to the needs of our audience.

K S What is the core soul of Košice?

L B Košice is a charming historical student city, surrounded by stunning nature. It is a true melting pot between East and West. My wife perfectly captured it when she borrowed a term from David Lynch: "Wild at Heart." That is Košice in a nutshell—unpredictable, raw, and full of passion, yet also conservative, cosmopolitan, and provincial all at once.

K S How did you turn a cinema into a community meeting place?

L B This developed very organically. People started gathering around the cinema, drawn in by the film selection and the cool, cozy bar. Now, we are getting more intentional about community-building, and it has become a significant focus of our professional efforts. We are focusing on uniting diverse groups. For some, it is one of the few chances to socialize and have a night out. But, just like the best things, it started off informally and spontaneously.

Fig. 2: Kino Úsmev's pop-up screenings bring movies to unique locations, like a riverside film picnic by the Hornád, combining the cinema experience with the natural beauty of Košice's surroundings.

Fig. 3, 4, 5: Záhradné Kino, operated by Kino Úsmev, is a beloved summer cinema hidden in Košice's historical center. Nestled between Hlavná 80 and Mäsiarska 37, it offers a unique open-air experience, screening timeless classics and art films during the warmer months.

K S What major changes have you seen in the community since you got involved?

L B   One of our main roles, aside from showing amazing new films, is to help people be more sensitive, more aware of those around them, and more reflective of themselves.

K S What have you learned over the years? How do you make change happen and overcome obstacles?

L B   In a recent talk about the current political turmoil, which is wreaking havoc on the cultural sector in Slovakia, I realized that since we started the cinema, we have been in a constant state of crisis. From borrowing money from family to get started, grinding hard to pay it back, surviving COVID, which nearly shut us down, enduring the energy crisis, and now navigating this political storm—it has been stressful non-stop. But, oddly enough, these challenges made us tougher. Our team grew stronger, we found new ways to keep going, and we started working more internationally. The one thing that never changed is our passion for film, for what we do, and for our values. What I have learned is that if you love what you

Fig. 6: Kino Úsmev offers a vibrant summer atmosphere with its outdoor terrace and street food park, making it a popular gathering spot for both locals and visitors.

do and have solid people around you, you can push through any bullshit that comes your way.

K S **You recognize the challenges facing the world, yet you focus on improving your community for the better. What keeps you optimistic?**

L B This might sound cliché, but it is the people. When I see individuals benefiting from our work—whether their quality of life improves or they are inspired to do better—it gives me a sense of purpose and motivation to keep going. That is the fuel for the fire.

K S **What do you think is the next step for change right now?**

L B We need to cut through the noise and all the crap and focus on finding the truth. In a world full of distractions and alternative facts, it is easy to lose sight of what really matters. We need to be more sensitive, more thoughtful, and more tolerant. And let us not forget, our planet is literally burning while we continue to talk. It is time to be more mindful and stop taking things for granted.

A conversation between   Barbara Meyer   & Karl Stocker

Creating *Something New* Because There Is No Solution

BARBARA MEYER is the Director of the Culture Centre S27—Art and Education in Berlin Kreuzberg. She grew up in Switzerland and studied fine arts at the Academy of Fine Arts Munich, later Art in Context at the Academic University of the Arts in Berlin. In 2006, she organized the campaign OFFENSIVE KULTURELLE BILDUNG, Offensive Cultural Education, a workshop conference on behalf of the artistic and cultural council Rat für die Künste. Until 2009, she managed the Berlin Fund for Cultural Education. In 2020, she launched the Initiative Urban Practice with a group of artists and architects. Barbara Meyer is a member of the Refugee Council Berlin.

CREATING SOMETHING NEW BECAUSE THERE IS NO SOLUTION

K S Why not start our conversation with a kind of ruminating and reflective throw-back on your life. Can you name a few defining moments that are important to you?

B M   All things considered, professionally as well as in private, I think I have taken some ordinary but also a fair share of odd paths to end up where I am today. I grew up near Lucerne, an area surrounded by mountain ranges. The region is buzzing with cultural and adventure tourism. In addition, there is a vast network of international musicians facilitating an impressive global exchange in music. I had the best of both worlds, living extremely close to the mountains while at the same time being able to tap into this colorful and busy world full of art and history. I believe this has shaped me immensely as a person.

My first ever job was in Sarnen. The canton is called Obwalden, a pastoral region with idyllic mountain ranges. I had accepted a position as a primary school teacher. Living there taught me a lot about the relationship between humans and space. In this case referring to the social as well as symbolic definition of the terms space and place. This environment, formed by mountains and valleys, defines and molds people's lives. Despite the harsh conditions on some of these rugged mountain roads causing commutes of more than an hour for some of the students, most of them managed to turn up to school every single day. My internships too were located far away from larger hubs. They were in tiny school buildings in remote locations somewhere in the mountains where they had to group together grades one to six. Basic arithmetic, reading, music—all this, while bracing snow and fog. Looking back on it today, I realize that in education, the concept of one managing and organizing everything was developed out of necessity.

This has shown me a lot. First and foremost, the solutions to specific issues often present alongside the problems themselves. There is no alternative but to find solutions. For instance, where I am right now, there are children and young adults who need access to education as quickly as possible. Facing this urgency, you suck it up and just do it. On the occasion that you run into trouble following a regular school schedule with your students, you adapt and create lesson and study plans yourself. This approach is especially important to me nowadays. We are confronted with a ton of kids, especially those coming from a migrant or refugee background, that cannot attend school simply due to a shortage of accommodation.

No one is willing to discuss that instead of waiting for offers and open spots, you have to take the initiative yourself. The necessity emerging from these deficits is often the key to innovation. This is an incredibly crucial driver of change. During my quite short-lived career as a teacher, I experienced a remarkably flexible and open education system in Switzerland. Unfortunately, this has changed noticeably. There are now a bunch of new regulations and a lot more bureaucracy than I encountered back then. As young teachers in the eighties, we were given a goal that had to be achieved by the end of the school year. Teaching material, how and where classes had to be taught, and methodological techniques were not as set in stone. We were given way more freedom to plan and approach our lessons and long-term targets. Even though the notion of project-based learning was a brand-new expression, no one was really interested in the label itself. Teachers there had been designing their lessons to be applicable, practical and relatable anyhow. This included things like turning forests into an interactive classroom, teaching geometry in the bicycle shop

108

Fig. 1: S27 Bildungsmanufaktur: collaborative team from the sixth-form college Hans Böckler, 2021

and organizing excavations in the parish's communal garden. In the hopes of sparking interest and achieving a steeper learning curve, the focus of these lessons was always to encourage the kids to see for themselves and not to be afraid of experimentation. Yet, which rooms, spaces and environments best support the process of discovery alongside learning and studying in regard to methods and curriculums? You just have to ask yourself one question really. What makes the most sense in terms of efficiency concerning study goals? Honestly though, the term project in project-based learning is actually to be criticized. Although it sounds fantastic in theory, in everyday school life it is more an exception to the rule. Trying to implement it on a regular basis is surprisingly hard given the strict curriculum and circumstances in schools. While the benefits are always welcome and amazing, it is really just a brief interruption to an otherwise inadequate and worn-out routine.

The project never has a long-term effect on the system since it is neither included in the budget nor in any future plans in general. Special projects are given a fun label plus an appealing design. Sadly, they merely hint at transformation and almost completely fail to address inclusion and participation. Obsolescence manages to survive even though its own definition states the opposite. Any terminology that would be associated with a reorientation

Fig. 2: Future market FALSCHER FISCH (FAKE FISH), Todosch Schlopsnies installation, 2022

in a crisis did not exist. Irregularity grants a kind of freedom to new ideas. As a result, it was possible to make hay while the sun shines and establish a permanent impact on day-to-day proceedings.

Recently, I have become more aware of this phenomenon. Innovative ideas, constantly working on provisional solutions and trying out new things without it bearing a particular label are strong indicators of change. We sometimes refer to them as clumsy things because that is sort of how they happen, by accident. In fact, the unknown, the new is being killed by pre-formulated targets and requirements with invitations to tender and applications for project funding.

Of course, Switzerland was not South Sudan, where there was an actual state of emergency at that time. Nevertheless, more often than not, it was absolutely unavoidable to improvise while teaching in this rough mountainous region and I genuinely enjoyed it.

After teaching for a year, I longed for change and gave the preliminary course at the School of Design in Lucerne a shot. I completed it and in retrospect, this phase was important and has deeply influenced my understanding of and approach to larger concepts. The old Bauhaus pre-requisite classes were designed like an obstacle course. It introduced me to trades like welding, carpentry, stonemasonry and the manufacturing process of garments to name a few. These are all crafts that allow you to be inventive and create while also learning to understand the techniques of the works. It is a quite straightforward learning space for studying aesthetics and design. Where I am now, we have been applying Bauhaus' basic educational theories and approach to pedagogy for ten years. Mostly in our Bildungsmanufaktur, a vocational training school in our youth center S27 that is open to everyone. The name roughly translates to "manufacturing education and knowledge", which is exactly what we are trying to do.

After the School of Design, I went to Munich to attend the Academy of Fine Arts. Right after arriving there, I thought about a change of course, and studying at the Faculty of Theology. These whimsical and fictional images and the ideas regarding the origin of the world as we know it, truthfully speaking the entire visual culture of Catholicism, has always fascinated me; when I was kid and as soon as I spent any time in the mountains. The corporation, which it is in my opinion, has always been problematic and has even become unacceptable. It was not meant to be and never stood a chance. I ended up staying at the academy where I studied fine art, public art and new artistic strategies. Gerd Winner was the supervisor and lecturer. After graduating with honors, I moved to Berlin.

The Art Academy made me happy in many ways, but I had a hard time establishing a reliable career that also suited me. I always thought, what a strange line of work. For about five years, you are constantly being told that there must be something ingenious about you, otherwise you would have never ended up in the sublime temple of the art world. However, there were countless times when I witnessed fellow students, mostly young people who had just left the academy, simply stepping into nothingness. There is a huge discrepancy between the expectation of this program and what is truly achievable afterwards. I have not seen a single solution to this problem! How dare society forgo so many young people! Despite having studied the arts for numerous years, putting a lot of effort into it, they struggle with feeling and sometimes even being looked at as not enough, unqualified and incompetent for actual jobs. As a result, they end up frustrated and depressed because they are not able to win or at least make a name for themselves in any competitions

CREATING SOMETHING NEW BECAUSE THERE IS NO SOLUTION

"I consider art markets to be a *one-way street*. Once I had become aware of that during my studies, I have been committed to never ever setting foot anywhere near that part of the *art world* ever since."

or simply cannot find a gallery. Graduating from this program feels unexpectedly insipid and mundane. In contrast to how much art studies are being hyped and how grandiose they are supposed to be, the ending and what comes right after is profoundly banal. Art studies are terribly underdeveloped and in addition to that a disaster from an economic point of view.

I consider art markets to be a one-way street. Once I had become aware of that during my studies, I have been committed to never ever setting foot anywhere near that part of the art world ever since. Finding alternatives was hard though. You had to create them yourself. In fact, university had actually prepared me for that. Courses as well as practical workshops about the science of aesthetics and even ideas for collaborative productions were sparse or lacking utterly. This is an issue I see time and time again. The understanding of aesthetic judgment and thus our actions are essential in today's everyday world, however they are not included in any form whatsoever in our standard educational system across the board. Daycare centers, schools, vocational training schools and universities would all benefit from it. Therefore, I was in search of an artistic practice that is able to connect with people and focuses on design tasks that transform systematic structures.

There should be abstract compositions of any works in progress, a bit like study group projects, that show characters that play an important role in society, plus help predict and plan change.

After some time, I moved to Berlin and continued my academic education at what was then known as the Cultural Center for Pedagogy and Post-Secondary Education at the former Academic University of the Arts, the precursor of today's Institute for Art in Context at the Berlin University of the Arts. At that time, the institute was quite lively and buzzing. It was well connected to the city. Prior to the Bologna Process, students were running several exciting and long-term projects. They had to learn how to set those up as if it was their actual job in real life; applying for funding first in order to arrange, display and put together anything in museums, abandoned buildings or public spaces like decrepit neighborhoods.

In 1991, I finished my studies and signed a short-term contract as a lecturer at the Academic University of the Arts in Berlin. At the same time, I founded a small project-oriented company, the Short Art GbR, together with Carolina Kecskemethy, a fellow artist. We showed up with an open studio concept at various spots in the city and gave teenagers a chance to participate. To begin with, I had not been able to provide

112

Fig. 3: Women's group LUZI: rug tufting with Katja Schmidt at the urban lab FALSCHER FISCH (FAKE FISH), 2023

an actual room for a studio, but I did get lucky eventually and was able to use a larger common room in the basement of a refugee shelter free of charge. That was right here in Berlin, in Treptow. This idea of an open studio that I managed to establish there laid a conceptual basis that is prevalent to this day.

The transition from Munich to Berlin was pivotal in terms of self-development. Munich and Switzerland had too much in common. Berlin, on the other hand, was rather kaput before the Wall came down. Poverty was visible in various aspects, and I was surprised by the sheer number of damaged buildings. History lessons in Switzerland covered very little about Germany, like living conditions in a divided and physically separated country. Initially, I was somewhat alienated by this highly militarized environment enforcing checkpoints and inspections. Despite being deterred by all this, I was fascinated by the open space plus the fallow farmland that made the city special. Berlin was like

Fig. 4: Street view of Sonnenallee: shop signs from the tapestry workshop with Federica Teti, 2023

Fig. 5: Platz*da! EL DORFO, S27, the young days of Urban Practice, 2023

a big construction site. Even today, you will find a few areas and a general vibe among certain scenes and districts that reflect this open space. In order to try anything that had not been done before, all you had to do was show initiative and Berlin made it possible.

The cooperation at the institute facilitated an amazing framework and network that made it possible to easily get in touch with administrative organizational structures. This was especially useful when applying for permits regarding any projects in public areas. I organized a large event tent for a banquet at Bahnhof Zoo, a railway station in Charlottenburg, Berlin. The idea was to have a festive dinner in connection with a public workshop. This was all realizable with input from Claes Oldenburg and in cooperation with the NGO Bahnhofsmission, a charity offering help in every larger railway station across Germany. We had to persuade numerous project partners like the Berlin Homeless Charity and the Health Department in order to have them participate and be included in the planning. Since this was all new to them and harder to grasp, we needed to put in a lot more effort. Taking risks, our cut-and-try approach, even being daring at times did teach us so much, most importantly, that it is possible to change and transform omnipresent rigid structures. In this particular example, I believe the benefits of using public space as a platform for social functions were just too convincing.

Evidently, the second degree I pursued in Berlin differed from the one I completed in Munich. It focused on practice-based learning and was just a more applied course overall. Fortunately, this opened doors for me that did not lead to the art market.

Ever since I started my journey as an art student, the gap between fine and applied arts has lured me in and grabbed my attention. Is social design a form of applied arts? When you apply something, can it be experimental at the same time? The arts became far more candid and freer once they were not bound by contracts and jobs anymore. I mean, ever since photography has been invented, artists had to radically reinvent themselves and change gears, now that the traditional client was not the same anymore or completely disappeared. Aside from this absolutely spectacular freedom that had started to expand, criticism arose: Why do artists even work? What do they work towards? Who is hiring them? We have to move away from this way of thinking, it supports an outdated construct. This image of a client has to be looked at from a whole different angle! It is us. It is our society. It is everyone.

Imagination, changing perspectives and outlining visions are not meant to be privileges solely reserved for artists. If a troubled world manages to make society reevaluate, the fine and applied arts will start to blend. Collaborations will resemble research projects. Rethinking and taking another look at the definition of applied art is long overdue. This is super relevant to what I am doing now. We are working on communication design, processes of change in any shape or form and social interaction in general. These are all instruments that define public life and communities. This has-been perception of application in the art scene can be reexamined in a more experimental way, like the approach urban practice is taking.

The disintegration of the disparity between applied and fine art enables plenty. Separation of those two is just not paramount, and I even think it does not really matter that much. Every piece of fine art that is not exhibited in public gets locked in a basement. While it does not do any harm there, it is of no use either. I do not want to diminish or offend the fine arts, but it is true that the applied arts are more relevant to my work. Splitting funding according to categories widens the disparity and furthermore hinders creativity since you have to fit the mold and abide by the regulations when you apply. I advocate for diverse collaborations, including intercultural ones, and loosening those strict definitions. Applied arts are not just exhibits and art collections.

K S Have you ever actually worked as an artist yourself or have you always been more engaged in the conceptual field where you inspire projects, come up with theories and concepts, envision the future, develop visions and try to implement those?

B M I have always painted and drawn a lot, but I have never wanted a typical career where one owns a studio, organizes exhibitions and participates in competitions. My painting career was severely shaken by my twin sons. Frankly speaking, the two were just better at it than me. I am actually pretty happy with my job because I create and look at my work as conceptual art. It is like an actual research lab. It allows me to try different methods and ideas among colleagues, friends and oodles of kids and young adults from all over the world. Working in the applied sector of aesthetic studies grants an enormous amount of creative freedom and I fully enjoy it!

Fig. 6: Studio Karfi Collection at Fashion Week 2022 with Philip Crawford

However, my development was not linear. I had to deal with a family emergency in the early two-thousands. This required me to have a reliable income, which meant leaving the art world and my precarious job. For about five years I worked for an educational company that focused on projects I had no experience in. The Trade Association had just created room for a new vocational training program where graduates can officially call themselves event managers afterwards. For this new program, I was the one developing the study plan. Even though the world of finance and associations was not something I felt passionate about, I was able to learn a lot again. After being in constant communication with administration offices, businesses and the Chamber of Commerce and Industry, I could see the link between education, economics and socioeconomic segmentation. It is crazy to see how your country of origin, heritage and social background determines your chances and risks in society.

These experiences were certainly critical when my work was not affiliated with any school anymore. There was no more buffer zone, but I was able to use what I had picked up to good effect when I launched publicly accessible educational projects that were running for several years. Those were for everyone, there was no entry exam or requirements you had to meet in order to be admitted. Combining education with art forms is what I aspired to achieve. Those years I spent in the economic sector, dealing with the regulations surrounding vocational training were exhausting and honestly speaking, took the wind out of my sails.

Receiving a job offer from the Berlin Arts Council in Campaign Management was just in time and saved me from despair. Offensive Cultural Education for Berlin was the title of the new program they had just developed. It was intended as a form of protest against the recent removals of several school subjects related to art. The aim was to spark a visionary cooperation between artists and schools. Having various artistic directors on board proved to be a bonanza for the project. In the course of this, I was able to initiate an official grant for the state of Berlin. While I am glad it all worked out in the end, I experienced a lot of ups and downs and encountered a few surprises here and there in the process of it all. It was a challenging task since installing any new financial support turned out to be a complex undertaking with more than enough hurdles. In a way, it had the same effect as project-based learning, and I benefited from it in the long run. I went down the rabbit hole of authorization legislation and completely immersed myself in the world of juridical terms, bills and regulations. In 2009, I left the Berlin Project Fund for Arts and Cultural Education and became the Director of the art center Schlesische27.

"I do like to call it a lab because it is just really *a great cultural center* where the focus of aesthetic studies and education is practice-based and applied, which is exactly what I have always wanted to do."

All of these additional experiences turned out to be extremely helpful, I refer to them as my bag of goodies I collected over the years. Carrying it with me allows me to further develop the art center I am running. Understanding harmony and balance when trying to put together anything while never stopping to be curious and to experiment with conceptual ideas is quintessential. In addition to that, being able to deal with

Fig. 7: Bildungsmanufaktur, 2023

bureaucracy, financial decisions, staying in close contact with businesses, politics and the authorities is a huge part of the job. In order to cut the mustard, I need to be able to have the skill set to manage both of these distinct aspects. Considering the fact that all projects and any work we do here have to be wholly financed by third-party funding, I cannot go without knowing the ins and outs of fund management policies. On top of that we have to face challenges from immigration authorities regarding our work with refugees. Some of our employees themselves have a lot of psychological baggage to carry due to traumatic events they encountered while fleeing their country; some so severe it does restrict and limit their everyday life in a lot of ways. I am genuinely glad they wound up with us. Not only can we help and be there for one another, but by being part of such an incredible international team, we have been able to create a network of artists, NGOs and partners all around the globe.

In a way, the issues and topics I first bumped into when I started my open studio in that basement have remained ubiquitous in my life to this day. My work is an amalgamation of conceptual art, urban practice, socioeconomic design on one hand and immigration laws on the other hand. We are constantly confronted with challenging situations and emergencies. We got it all here under one roof: the essentialness of meeting basic human needs alongside discussions about design and education.

Fig. 8: Sitting Conference,
Monobloc Lab with Michael Wolke, 2024

CREATING SOMETHING NEW BECAUSE THERE IS NO SOLUTION

"Since tragedies are an unfortunate part of emergencies, they require us to *be more inventive*. Coming up with new things in times of crises is deeply rooted in *the origin of art* as well. You have to *trust the process* since the result might not be visible, not tangible yet."

Emergencies on a small scale, like in our facility, and on a larger scale globally speaking, show us that things have to be done ad hoc. It is about taking initiative without receiving instructions or being asked to do them by the authorities. Solutions are needed now, and it is urgent. The cultural consultant and filmmaker Michael Schindhelm uses the term adhocracy in reference to imminent challenges regarding cultural management as well as global states of emergencies. Looking back at the recent Covid pandemic for instance, where we had to deal with immense uncertainty, our rigid structures were not capable of properly withstanding the impact of such catastrophes. Dealing with problems like this requires us to be more flexible in order to make the best of it. We need change.

This is the responsibility I deem important, hence the values our institution represents. Every day, we notice an increase in poverty and insecurities people face here in the city of Berlin. The housing crisis is not getting any better and the cost of living is rising. We provide the stage for all of those people to come together; it affects us directly. Our society and living conditions are changing way too quickly. Right now, there are zero solutions that are fast and truly feasible.

Since tragedies are an unfortunate part of emergencies, they require us to be more inventive. Coming up with new things in times of crises is deeply rooted in the origin of art as well. You have to trust the process since the result might not be visible, not tangible yet. Just like an artist's painting. This idea captivated me to a great extent, which eventually led me to philosophy. I started reading about different theories about utopias and their potential to one day become reality.

I cherished Ernst Bloch's thoughts and ideas, in particular his attention to what he described as an effigy of an authentic presence. Admittedly, it is a strange concatenation of words, but I do think it is on the nose. According to him, future events are being foreshadowed. It is on us to find its outline and try different approaches in order to predict what is forthcoming. This was not exclusively appertaining to the arts. It reads more like a task he assigned all of us to work on. We all have to play the cards we are dealt to achieve the next best thing and never stop aspiring for change.

While working on construction sites and in workshops, we use this axiom as guidance. We are not certain where the journey is headed, but we have hopped on the bandwagon, nonetheless.

Fig. 9: S27 group Kochinsel (Kitchen Island) at urban lab FALSCHER FISCH (FAKE FISH), 2023

The arts provide and present diverse tools and spaces. When things get difficult, they lend a helping hand. Utilizing the arts when faced with unrest and uncertainty can be encouraging. We have attempted to apply this concept of foreshadowing by having a go at various drafts and tackling projects from all kinds of angles, trying to figure out where they might lead to. If you look at it like a strategic game, there are a few obvious influences that play a role in development and change. I would like to refer to them as pawns. They are pulling the strings on a social, urban, ecological and economic level. Experimenting with those can result in the identification of pivotal key qualities that sustainable transformation needs as a means to be propelled forward.

I highly recommend this method. Trust me, try it! I can give you an example. In 2014, the majority of young people who turned up at our art center as refugees were prohibited by law from taking up any employment. But our workshops made it possible to start a kind of project reality. So, five young men started building furniture. We were thinking, huh, they could actually become great furniture makers! What if they used the aesthetic background of a woodworking shop, like an actual manufacturer, to present their work and implement the concept of an open workshop where everyone could stop by and observe them at work. This would create an illusion, an image that resembled an actual company to the point where it would be difficult to distinguish it from an actual one.

Eventually those five men from West Africa, with the support of two of our designers, founded a furniture making business. The company was called CUCULA—Refugees Company for Crafts and Design. This was a daring experiment. In the sense of setting an example, it was incredibly effective, but the undertaking was extremely arduous and risky for everyone involved. Seeing a successful company that was created by refugees, which was not legal, did pose a few questions. Why is it not allowed? Why should it not be allowed if it is doable? Precisely this act of defiance, which of course attracted the media's attention, contributed to the heated debate about the right to work for refugees and asylum seekers in 2015.

Claiming CUCULA alone would have been enough to change the law would be pretentious and presumptuous. Letting a team from West Africa start a design company to build chairs, tables and cabinets

Fig. 10: Les Microbes, installation at the set of the film with Matze Görig, 2024

according to plans and blueprints from Enzo Mari left a mark on theories and visions of what a future could look like. Impressive aesthetic experiments and strategies like these can originate from applied arts like socio- and socioeconomic design.

Every now and then I consider doing a bit more research on marketing strategies and propaganda. I believe it would be refreshing and interesting to have people like us, with a background in urban practice, social studies, socioeconomics and aesthetic education, take a gander at these areas. Marketing promoters construct images that convey lifestyles and create certain atmospheres. Their goal is to reach a critical moment, a tipping point, that suggests a different perception. At this point I would like to mention Edward Louis Bernays. Bernays, born into a family of psychologists, was an American expert of public relations. He deliberately used aesthetic strategies in advertising, which later in history, were also adopted as guidelines for propaganda and manipulation. The capitalist and political use and abuse of role models is a hot potato; highly controversial and rightfully criticized. Goebbels, the Minister for Public Enlightenment and Propaganda for the German Third Reich, admired Bernays' work. United Fruit Company, notorious for exploitation and toxic pesticide scandals on their plantations, was able to stay ahead of the competition and maneuver their company to the top by rebranding the Chiquita banana with Bernays' help. For the first time in history, an organic product turned into a market sensation and all of that just because of a small blue sticker on a yellow banana peel. Bernays' took the banana out of its natural environment by aesthetic intervention and introduced it to the market. This overhaul had detrimental consequences; it turned the world into a discount store.

However, experimenting with shifting images remains an intriguing motor for social change. As a way of utilizing these procedures for fundamental transformations, I believe they have to be employed in all areas of society.

From time to time, in our art center S27, we were able to assist specific projects in initiating spin-offs like smaller companies, start-ups and associations.

> "Anyone who is entirely perceived as poor by society needs *a change of perspective*. Activities and hobbies that can be turned into a profession lay the groundwork for a *change of image* and *self-employment*."

Dignified photos and reports that showcase self-confident refugees and immigrants who have started their own businesses knock the bottom out of those denouncing images created by the extreme right. We all know how opprobriously blatant they are. Spreading like wildfire, nonetheless.

They also make use of images. In search of a better reputation and a unique self-image, they are trying to stand out instead of feeling invisible. People who have been laid off and simultaneously dropped out of all social networks, are looking for images that help them piece together a lost self-efficacy and regenerate a purpose in life. The far right in their fight against the "others", mostly referring to immigrants, heavily push their political party platform and reach maximum engagement by creating extreme posts and posters along with protest songs and chants.

These days, perceived devaluation caused by a weakened or lost introspection, is making people sick and eases them into an ultraconservative, rightist political position. This is especially prevalent in areas where industries and manufacturers have been declining to the point of closure. Instead of progress, there is an increase in the demand for unemployment benefits and social welfare. Not just the lack of money though, on the contrary, the financial safety net of inheritance has made people void and reduced their existence to isolated recipients of benefits. While those two groups often share regressive and traditionalist opinions, one's clearly louder and more active, while the other one is more of a silent, passive participant.

Doomed is the attitude of getting accustomed to being a consumer instead of a producer in many regards. Democracy and democratic societies take the fall for it. My generation has gradually lost touch with the idea of being part of any manufacturing processes.

Supply and scarcity are an example of balanced dualism. Therefore, it is nowhere near surprising that we experience an increase in extreme, antisocial and aggressive forms of expression. Creating an impact by assigning themselves roles and receiving validation by drawing attention when kicking up a fuss.

In 2018, the whimsical and peculiar Federal Ministry of the Interior was put into action. Despite countless programs and

Fig. 11: Street view of Sonnenallee: shop signs from the tapestry workshop with Federica Teti, 2023

events, they have not been very successful in achieving their main goal, promoting a more patriotic identification with Germany. Where do they offer an interior platform, a homeland, for cooperation and teamwork?

"One thing is certain though. The world is given as is, but *we can change* and *improve* it. That is the good news. Design labs and workshops are part of the *sine qua non* that lay the first stone when it comes to change."

K S What keeps you optimistic these days?

B M A lot actually. It is the simple, everyday moment that boosts optimism. I love going for a swim in between a nice run around Lake Grünewald and then just jogging through the forest in my swimsuit on my way back home. The fact that I can run through the forest half-naked proves to me that there is always a way even if there is nothing left. This is a blissful way of interpreting life, and it brings me joy. Optimistically speaking, one could conclude: Cutdowns are fun. Reduction is fun. Limitations are fun. It is not lost on me that this definitely sounds downright sarcastic. Most people experience the sudden lack of things as a terrible threat. Encountering hard times and living in poverty is awful, but there is always at least one moment where you can catch a glimpse of the glimmer of possible change.

Emergencies are completely depleting us of any sense of normality. Everything changes. Exactly because of the sudden collapse, we are forced to take the bull by the horns, we have no other choice but to muster the courage to defy the odds. Who knows, we might find an open door or two amongst the debris.

Where rules collapse, unmanageable situations arise and cracks appear, that is where the importance of the creation of commons becomes evident. Ensuring that shatter belts, neighborhoods that have not been gentrified, and abandoned buildings are not snatched up by slum lords like large investors. The power and the courage of so many of our activists can make a difference. While this sounds amazing, it is a herculean task since obstacles along the way are unavoidable. With the decline and withdrawal of the familiar though, incredibly creative situations arise alongside unexpectedly favorable conditions which accommodate social development.

Every day, I encounter these chances. Earlier I mentioned the shortage of school places. There are about 80 teenagers with refugee status showing up at our doors on a daily basis. Many of them wait several months for a spot. We have called countless schools and demonstrated in front of the Senate Administration for Education, but there is no end in sight. So, recognizing this as an emergency, we sat down and outlined the definitions and functions of schools, education and curriculums. How can we create an educational system that is adaptable and flexible and regards diversity as a great resource?

Let us rethink school and stop treating it like a construction site. We have launched an initiative called WELTSCHUL-HAUS. It roughly translates to global school. Outside of traditional schools, we have created classrooms and structures that combine teaching and learning on a more experimental level. Together with older refugees and teachers in our community, we built space for study groups, workshops and study labs. All of this is based on an interdisciplinary approach.

CREATING SOMETHING NEW BECAUSE THERE IS NO SOLUTION

Teaching here is multilingual in every subject. Languages carry ideas and wisdom that could be applied in this new diverse environment. Everyone feels free to explore new ideas together. We treasure our capital of knowledge that grows every minute with the help of our international and intercultural community.

We see ourselves as a kind of sect. Ha! Excuse me, that was a typical joke from Silesia. You may not believe it, but we are actually really into traditional forms and archaic terminology. We love to look at them in a different light, interpret, amend, adjust and convert them. Where does the master-apprentice relationship come from, what are its justifications, how can we reinterpret primary school and kindergarten. There are a bunch of old-fashioned terms that sound so weird, they create a million random images at once! If you are interested, I can name a few in German just to paint a picture. There is Lehrstuhl, Störbereitschaft and Gymnasialempfehlung. Super strange if you take them out of context, right? Unfortunately, the bizarreness does not translate into the English language.

Generally speaking, coming back to a form of education that might be feasible within our system, I believe that a middle school for everyone might work out considering the increasingly international student body.

Systemically, our organization is not at all concerned with withdrawing or isolating ourselves. Imagine the system and structures we are trying to change as a large cargo ship that has come to a halt. We are trying to make some noise, swimming up and down the hull, doing somersaults on the deck to see how we could remodel and fix the engine. That is how we envision ourselves. As artists. It is good. It fits.

Fig. 12: S27 Community, ROTE HALLE in Kreuzberg, 2023

A conversation between Ola Fransson & Christina Hedin

Does Fear Stand In The Way
Of Change?

OLA FRANSSON is the manager of Naturum, where he inspires and teaches visitors by showing the interactions between society and nature on a local level. He has worked on the creation of several exhibitions where he was responsible for the initial idea, the execution, and the final display. He is also one of the founders of Nature's Best Sweden, an organization for sustainable eco tourism. Additionally, Ola is an analyst and active in the culture, art and crafts community.

C H You have thought a lot about creating change. How are your thoughts evolving?

O F It is obvious that the methods we have used so far present challenges. Until now, we have placed too much faith in the idea that scientific facts alone will be enough to create change. Humanistic knowledge, and to some extent the practical knowledge available, have not been given sufficient space in the work of change. Since debate and discussion occur on many different levels, it becomes difficult to formulate coherent questions and answers.

Another issue is that those of us who want to share a message may often think, "We are the ones who are right and virtuous." However, this may not always be the case. We must approach opposition with even greater humility. I believe this fosters more respect and opens the door for more constructive dialogue. I have learned that it is acceptable to be wrong, as it is part of the process. However, deliberately causing harm is never tolerable.

The technical solutions have been available since the early nineties. Addressing these solutions to create change is not the real challenge. Getting caught up in technical and detailed discussions usually leads to nowhere. On the other hand, reasoning and talking with each other about our core values and what we believe is important in our lives and for future generations. While discussions about how we are going to change can occur in parallel, debating whether to prioritize raising grazing livestock, or having electric cars, electric bikes, hybrid cars, or no cars at all—and getting bogged down in such details—will not help much at this stage. These are practical issues that can be resolved more easily if our values and norms shift. Until we are willing to do that, technical discussions will remain secondary.

Fig. 1: To have all your gear in order is essential in the mountains.

We need to reassess what we value. While we talk about sustainability, I prefer to talk about balance. In the Sami worldview, balance is emphasized over sustainability, but balance naturally leads to sustainability. The economic mindset that dominates today is a cultural construct. We have been taught that money brings happiness, but can we imagine a world where something else holds greater importance? We choose to believe that wealth is the ultimate measure of worth. But is it really necessary to assign value if we are the ones measuring it? When should subjectivity take precedence over objectivity? Norms are crucial, but it is also important to question them. Unfortunately, we have been too afraid to do that in recent decades.

We must change our culture, and to do so, we need to understand what it truly means to be human. What is our culture? What does it mean to be human? Empathy is part of our identity. In consequence, we depend on one another. However, at the same time, we struggle to manage interactions in groups larger than about 30 people. Beyond this threshold, in stressful conditions, conflicts arise, and socially, we are not equipped to handle such complexity. So, we have to infuse this awareness into the system.

To answer your question succinctly, the most important factor in driving change is probably finding ways to get people to pursue transformation that encourages long-term sustainability. We achieve this by helping them realize how this will personally benefit them.

We often have the illusion that we are rational in the context of classic political and economic debates. However, it does not take long to observe that we are not always pragmatic. At the same time, we are frequently labeled as inherently greedy. Modern research, such as the work of Frans de Waal, shows that we are actually born empathic. This challenges the notion that facts will always guide our choices, as emotions do play a role. We are primarily guided by various innate functions, with rationality being just among many. For instance, our need to avoid ostracism and belong to a group can often lead to seemingly irrational decisions.

C H You have told us that we view nature in different ways. Could you further describe that?

O F It is important to clarify what we mean by the term nature, so we are all on the same page. Nature is often regarded as a straightforward and universally understood concept, but it is not that simple. Assuming that everyone shares the same perspective can lead to unnecessary disagreements and misunderstandings. In the worst cases, this lack of clarity can slow down progress towards bringing our planet into balance.

In conversations, I will sometimes find that the other person has a completely different perspective of nature than I do. It is not surprising, then, that communication falters. I often find myself debating the concept in my mind and getting nowhere.

To address this, I wanted to create a communication tool that facilitates a more effective dialogue by having a clear definition of nature.

I was raised with the idea that we are not merely part of our environment, but that we are nature. My father, who was raised by his grandparents in a remote place in northern Sweden, grew up without roads, electricity, or modern conveniences–following old traditions. He was the one who helped me see that the same elements we find in trees are integral to our composition.

He was also the one who taught me that if you put food in your mouth, it gives you sustenance and later leaves you as a new form of fertilizer to the ground. Blurring the lines between nature and ourselves. If you do something that is bad for the land, is that not the same as shooting yourself in the foot?

I often wonder why others seem to have a disconnected perception of the outside world. My colleague and I spent a year discussing these different interpretations. These conversations eventually developed into an exhibition titled Your Nature? Who Is In The Way: The Road, or The Moose?

Fig. 2: Telling stories is the best way to learn about nature.

I explored the perspectives on nature to help myself and others make sense of it. An ulterior motive I had was that this exhibition would spark new ideas and inspire fresh ways of thinking. The philosophical debate about where we are now and what kind of future we envision was missing. One of several problems that we could solve is the fragmentation in society. For example, we focus on protecting a few patches of land and use that as a way to ease our collective guilt. But could it be more important to have a holistic view, rather than solely protecting isolated segments?

When people visit the exhibition, they tend to start with the standpoint they feel most familiar with, interpreting the others through that lens. It is tempting to view your opinion as superior and criticize others. Questioning your own beliefs can be challenging, and it is easy to react with aversion. This process often takes time. My role is to provide the opportunity for open dialogue in order to overcome the obstacle of unfamiliarity. In order to ease into a conversation, I use motivational interviewing techniques that were originally developed in healthcare, allowing for change in destructive habits.

There are four different ways of viewing nature, in my opinion. The original vantage point is that boundaries do not exist. The land and air are free. Adapting to conditions is highly valued. There is no definition of nature, it simply is ubiquitous. We do not regard ourselves as a mere fragment of this environment, instead, we are intertwined in all that exists. There is connection in composition. There is a great deal of practical knowledge about the landscape, but less about how it functions. This is how people create their own explanations for phenomena, such as the Northern Lights being spirits dancing.

The second is the scientific outlook, where we divide, sort, structure, and delimit. With this view, it is important to achieve your goals, while adaptation is not relevant. Humanity places itself at the center of everything, coining the term nature, observing it from a distance, and analyzing it to uncover the origin of it all. This helps obtain sustainable truths, with natural phenomena explained through science, and the dancing spirits fade away.

The third is an economic analysis, where we rely on the landscape and what nature provides. Concepts such as ecosystem services and green infrastructure are invented to remind us that we depend on natural resources. The word economy itself means housekeeping. Failing to manage resources can create wounds that cannot heal. Earth is our capital. Investing sustainably and only living off the returns is an innocuous way of successfully going about this approach. Yet, taking out more than the paid interest slowly diminishes our original funds. In reality, this means using our ecosystem, our home, as payment. The fact that we are living in the Anthropocene becomes evident when you examine this perspective.

The fourth is an idealistic notion. The sun is always shining on Instagram, so we crave perfection in reality. We take photos, record moments, edit them to seem flawless and post them to social media. Nature becomes a status symbol of success, the facade of an untouched wilderness is a mere accessory, and it is only for our pleasure.

I think that these four views of nature should have an equal share of the conversation. We need more research and vision, but we also need to know our roots. After all, natural resources make our life as it is possible.

I was raised with the idea that we should take care of the forest because it sustains us. For me, this connection is fundamental. At the same time, I am like everyone else—I also want to go cycling and climbing. Enjoying the romanticized image of nature resonates with me too.

In the area where I work, there are popular hiking trails that have become so heavily used that tourism had to be restricted and redirected to various other locations. However, many tourists do not want to be limited and accept that they cannot simply invade everywhere they want to, just for a photo opportunity. They do not realize or care that nature needs to recover. I cannot help but try to theorize how these perspectives differ from my father's philosophy.

Today, we provide so-called ecosystem services to put an economic value on a piece of land and I believe this is the biggest downfall of us as humans. Have we not already understood that we need worms in the soil? Why do we feel the need to emphasize that worms have a value?

A few years ago, there was a process to designate the area where I work as a national park. That made it clear to me that the original and the academic scientific view do not align. The traditional view sees everything as interconnected and indivisible, while the academic perspective seeks to fragment, divide, and systematize.

The strength—and risk—of the traditional view is that where there are no answers, people invent them based on what seems reasonable. That is how we like to do it. We do not accept uncertainty. While this approach can work, it can also lead to disastrous consequences.

You cannot negotiate with nature. It has its laws, and we have to follow them. However, in order to do that, our attitudes towards nature need to change. With the right attitude, the future will no longer feel like a threat; it will be something to look forward to again.

C H You meet many people at your work. How do you approach them?

O F There are many different people, and I want them to feel comfortable in approaching me, though I do not always succeed in that—depending on how tired I am. But I think it is important not to talk to people, but to talk with them. I use my own stories, which can be a little long-winded, but I think they are important. Tourists must understand what is at stake, yet I want them to enjoy their experience.

While I love sharing my thoughts, I have no intention of converting anyone I meet. Who knows if I am right or not, but I do have the overarching goal to give people the opportunity to take responsibility.

If you want a person to listen, they need to feel respected. I achieve that by meeting them where they are, no matter their age or title. Talking to kids is actually a lot of fun because they are a lot more intuitive. I am genuinely happy when people engage in the conversation, it shows they are listening. Sometimes it happens that it just does not click, so I let those interactions go. It is not worth anyone's time and energy. Personally, I try to work on not taking offense in my professional environment.

C H Have economic values been more important in our society?

O F I am not sure if monetary economics has become more important, but we certainly talk about it more. I noticed that other values have disappeared. How much money do you really need to feel content though? And how long does it last? We need to create incentives to rethink the relationship between finances and happiness. Concepts such as ecosystem services did not exist 30 years ago.

"You cannot negotiate with nature. It has its *laws*, and we have to follow them. However, in order to do that, our *attitudes* towards nature need to change. With the right attitude, the future will no longer feel like a *threat*; it will be something to look forward to again."

I grew up in an environment that did not adhere to any particular political ideology. But one of the finest words I know is solidarity, also towards strangers. Sadly, that word is hardly used in any form of debate today. Perhaps we could use it synonymously with care.

When I was twelve years old, I once wrote, "we plus we plus them = solidarity." I don't know if that is true, but I still carry it in my mind. It is fulfilling to help others—even if you will never meet the person again.

C H Something else that I also strongly associate with you is your work with tracks. Why should we read tracks?

O F The most obvious example is to look at animal tracks, but it does not stop there. Everything that happens leaves a trace that can be deciphered. Learning to read these requires knowledge.

Upon closer inspection, you can determine its origin and predict where the next step might be. By learning how to read these tracks, we can gain a deeper understanding of the past and the future

C H What are your thoughts on climate change?

O F Some say, "only weed smoking vegans believe in climate change." What does that tell me? Well, it is a track that points in an understandable direction—fear. It is a rational person making a very stupid statement. But where does this fear come from? If you are in the phase of negating everything, it requires energy to generate change because you are comfortable where you are. You do not want to leave this cozy place. This fear is deeply rooted in us, and because of that, we have to support each other. As individuals, we need help to deal with changes—we cannot do it alone. I think this mindset is integrated in our culture; it is not just a phase.

We find ourselves in a situation where owning up to our actions feels daunting. We have been conditioned to view it as something we should not feel good about. While some people find it easier to take the blame, most are capable of mustering the courage to do so. However, admitting fault is rarely celebrated in today's world. We need to change this and make personal integrity the norm once more. True adulthood begins when you are willing to own your choices.

My thoughts on environmental destruction and climate change, especially in terms of how we cut down our forests, is that we are sawing off the branch we are sitting on. That is why you have to trust institutions to make decisions, because I do not think we can easily do it as individuals. A clear and decisive leadership is required. Unfortunately, I do not see that today. While it may take away power from us humans, it is central to our survival. Our solidarity compels and enables us to do this.

During the COVID-19 pandemic, the authorities imposed strict restrictions to keep us safe, even though they were very intrusive. Fear did not get the better of the authorities' decisions; science prevailed, which shows the strength of that approach to nature. To reach people, presenting the facts is sometimes not enough. Many have to experience it firsthand in order to draw conclusions. Which is exactly what happened during the pandemic. Either we got sick ourselves, or our neighbors did. We understood that it was serious.

With global warming, the now common occurrence of floods can be used as an example to show that it is real, that we do face climate issues today. Journalists should stop minimizing it by saying that they do not know if these events are related. Why hide the obvious? Is it because you are personally afraid of it? It is the end of May right now, and we are melting in western Jämtland, where it is usually cold

at this time of year. What else could help be more cognizant about climate change? How will it be when many more people want to live here because it gets too hot in other countries?

Two years ago, I had a very interesting experience in Abisko, a small village in the far north of Sweden. We had gathered for a meeting with other managers who work in a Naturum, visitor centers with exhibitions in some of our national parks and nature reserves. All of them were well-versed in climate change and occupied by intense studies about the atmosphere and the impact an increasing amount of carbon dioxide can have.

The group joined Keith Larsson, an exceptional interpreter and Head of Research at the Abisko Scientific Research Station, to go out for an on-site discussion about climate change. Some people sighed, remarking that we already knew a great deal about it. Together, we ventured onto a bog, where we drilled holes into the ground to reach the permafrost. As we reached down and felt the frozen layer, he explained that just three meters away, the permafrost had disappeared, leaving only a hole now. That was three years ago. Three years ago! This will be gone next year. Half the group started crying. We have to do something! During the evening, as we reflected on this, I was a little surprised about the number of people that were emotional about it. Many of them were from the southern part of Sweden, where the signs of climate change are not as clear to see.

Underlined by this experience, we agreed to make an effort for the climate and our planet. Yet, over two years later, it has still not been launched. We have had a lot of meetings, but nothing has come of them. In the beginning, I said that I would give it three meetings, and if nothing much comes about, I am out. Unfortunately, this is exactly what has happened.

Fig. 3: The best coffee is served in the sunny snow.

> "We will be *forced to change*, and if we refuse, we will die—it is that simple. Nature will *remain*, even without us *humans*."

Some of them changed their minds, and others careers.

We had such great potential. A fantastic researcher with lots of resources was eager to collaborate with us, but things did not work out. So far, only one or two Naturum centers have done work related to climate change.

C H Do you think we spend enough time on analysis in our society?

O F Certainly not, especially not within institutions and administrations. Even if we invest time, we rarely take the necessary steps to follow up on it. I have lost count of how many evaluations I have written and yet, nothing has changed.

Evaluations and analyses are not the same. Surveys have been conducted and assessments have been made tens of thousands of times. How often do we take the time though to properly analyze our actions in order to learn from them as an organization?

In May, we face a recurring issue. Reindeer, during their sensitive calving season share the landscape with the last wave of backcountry skiers taking advantage of the lingering snow and sunny days. However, despite efforts to communicate to the skiers that they are disturbing the reindeer herding, we struggle to get through to them. Perhaps because they, just like snowmobile riders, have invested in expensive equipment, therefore they then feel compelled to make the most out of their trip.

How do we achieve meaningful change and encourage people to alter their behavior? Who could be an effective driving force? Do nature conservationists have to shoulder the responsibility of advocating for change, or do policymakers who can enforce regulations have to step up their game? Across the country, numerous signs urge people to change their behavior, but I doubt they do anything.

This brings us back to the start of this conversation. Both the problem and the solution start with us. It is said that you have to want to change, but I think this is not always right and depends on the circumstances. We will be forced to change, and if we refuse, we will die—it is that simple. Nature will remain, even without us humans.

C H This fear that you talk about, how do we overcome it?

O F Fear is as illogical as falling in love. There is no rationality to it; it just pops up. It arises when we face something unfamiliar or something beyond our control. Fear can be managed in different ways, both through our genetic wiring and through upbringing. If we took no risks at all, what would happen? Nothing? On the other hand, what would happen if we only took risks? Either way, everything would go to hell.

Fear is a part of a system; we need to step outside of our comfort zone and encourage people to be brave. It is easy to fear what we do not know. We look back and dream of the good old times. We know what we had, and we know what we have, but not what is to come. We need to help each other create new ideals, dreams, and visions—even though that can be unnerving and intimidating at times.

Being afraid and insecure is not dangerous when we move forward, but I do not want us to be ruled by it. I want us to be courageous and full of energy. Working together, we can influence each other's attitudes and inspire to make a difference—processes that give the future a chance. We can be the match that lights the fire. The fire that ignites action.

We need to accept our fear rather than run from it—acknowledgment helps. I have always been anxious. When I first spoke in front of a group, I was so nervous. Being completely broke, I had no choice, I needed the money. I analyzed the situation and realized that my low self-esteem made me think that I am not enough and nobody worth listening to. It helped me realize I was already at my lowest, and it could not get much worse than this. So, I went out and spoke. That day, I learned that bad feelings can be temporary, and now I know they usually pass. Even though I speak publicly every day, I still feel nervous sometimes. Through analysis I have found a method that works. Now I am starting to have a little more confidence, which makes it easier. What was once as hard as speaking to a group or walking out on a cliff is now manageable. Now I find that I feel rewarded with the connection of talking to others. It is important to evaluate our fears and try to understand them if we want to change anything.

Many instinctively react to new ideas by initially turning them down—due to worry or panic. It is hard to think clearly and listen to facts and information when we are frightened. Hence, we should prioritize dealing with our angst. This is not an easy challenge. One way that can get us out of our situation is reevaluating our fundamental values from a philosophical perspective. An open—and respectful—debate about this could lead to new ideologies.

Saying everything was better before is counterproductive. We need to move forward. We are doing something wrong and need to do it differently. While I support discussions about it, I do doubt that our brains are designed to find a perfect solution and execute it. I hear young people who feel that we are headed towards disaster—at full speed. Looking back, fixating on the past, means turning a blind eye to the road ahead. I see myself as the one telling them to turn around and look forward. However, it is important to keep an eye out for people paralyzed by fear. We have to watch out for each other. We have to either pull the brakes together; jump out of the thing that keeps moving dangerously fast; or steer towards a different direction, a different future. Our society, as it stands today, is over.

We need a new approach, a path toward meaningful change. While it is challenging, fear should not hold us back. If we work together, encourage, and empower one another, we can make this a reality. Success is within our reach. In truth, we have no alternative—we must act. While this is a word I seldom use, it underscores the urgency of our situation.

Despite the challenges, I remain hopeful. Our diverse cultures, with their varying norms, have contributed to the imbalance in our climate and the broader ecosphere. Yet norms and facts are not static; they can be reshaped. It is this understanding that fuels my optimism.

A conversation between Julia Kloiber & Karl Stocker

We Need To Ask The Right *Questions*

JULIA KLOIBER is a digital expert whose work lies at the crossroads of technology and society. She is the co-founder of the feminist organization Superrr Lab. Julia has launched several projects exploring how digital technology can benefit society, including the Prototype Fund, a funding program for public interest technologies, and the civic tech network Code for Germany. Her current work focuses on alternative future narratives for equitable digitalization. Julia Kloiber serves on the advisory board for the Federal German Digital Strategy, the Digital Service 4 Germany, and the German Postcode Lottery. She also writes a regular column for MIT Technology Review Germany.

K S **Starting with your life story, what contributed to your interest in sociopolitical changes in the context of of digitization, digitalization, and technology?**

J K Almost from the get-go, computers and new technologies were a part of my life. My father was a typical computer geek. And I mean this in the nicest way possible. As long as I can remember, he has always had a computer. In fact, in his hometown, he founded a computer club and offered computer courses. Evidently, I have been surrounded by tech since I was a child. The same goes for the internet. We were always up to speed with new developments in information technology. I can remember one time at Christmas, where I could barely hold my horses, thinking I would get my much-anticipated Barbie dollhouse. You can imagine my initial disappointment when I unwrapped my first ever computer.

In retrospect, however, getting in touch with technology at a very young age was an incredibly successful approach. When I was in middle school, they launched an introductory computer science class. The course was still in its infancy since the school launched it as a kind of experiment. I can recall our project—developing the school's website—very well. This was in the early nineties in Jennersdorf, a small town in the countryside in Southern Burgenland. Designing your first website, of course with the help of our computer science teacher, at the age of ten resonates with you. This initial fascination has stayed with me. Nothing is as effective in reaping the benefits of any training as hands-on work.

During my design studies, I started to wonder how these new digital tools can assist in outlining ideas, but I did not stop there. I further asked myself, what influence do they have on our society and democracy? In what way do they shape us? Thoughts like these piqued my curiosity. A lot of people have an optimistic, even utopian view on state-of-the-art technology. Constantly surrounded by this way of thinking, I started to ponder about perspectives we are missing out on when constantly looking through rose-tinted glasses. Who is left out? Whose needs are not taken into consideration? Which social groups might get harmed in the process? Where is the mainstream headed and who is being left behind? Technology can cause disadvantages and discrimination. Identifying and researching those gray areas that tend to get overlooked started to become my core interest in my field of study. I wanted to draw attention to things that usually are not looked at as much, but which are equally important in the grand scheme of things. By trying to grasp the issues, I was hoping to be able to improve them.

Enrolling in the Information Design program at JOANNEUM, the University of Applied Sciences in Graz, was just the next logical step. Did I choose this school because marketing and advertising appealed to me? Sure. Back then though, this study program and industry were a bit more prestigious and gatekept. Getting as close to it as possible was intriguing.

My parents were active in the community and volunteered a lot. Inspired by this, I have always known that I wanted to eventually focus my work on social aspects. In my case that meant, trying to figure out how to transform tools in a way that makes them useful and applicable in this area. While this sounds abstract in theory, let me illustrate this to make it a bit more tangible. I would take a look at advertising agencies and analyze how they market products with the purpose of applying those methods to achieve a social impact instead of a commercial one.

Fig 1: Behind the scenes, re:publica conference 2021, Berlin

Self-employment often appears less attractive when both parents are teachers, like mine. But instead of pushing this expectation of reaching tenure, my mom and dad gave us kids so much freedom and were supportive of our interests. They both grew up in a Catholic and Protestant, yet liberal social environment. Religion was not as important to them personally. While they were never part of the hippie movement at all, they did identify as progressive, socially critical and humanitarian. Born as children of the fifties, that was not an unusual thing to do for their generation. Considering their rather remote location somewhere in southern Burgenland, this was an act of rebellion.

K S Concerning your studies, was the JOANNEUM the only school you had settled on or were you eyeballing a few other universities and programs, too?

J K I had thought about the University of Applied Arts in Vienna, but quickly realized their education focuses heavily on art itself. While I consider anything artistic to be valuable and exciting, it just was not what I wanted for myself. I have always been more interested in practical approaches that allowed me to take a gander at different branches within a field of study before deciding which one I wanted to direct my attention to and pursue further. Honestly, the portfolio that the university in Graz had published was just really good and convinced me. It listed a raft of courses and projects that students could all participate in.

After graduating with a bachelor's degree, I topped it off with a graduate program. I did take a little break in between though. During this time, I moved to Berlin. For three years, I worked for an agency that followed the concept of guerrilla communication. They used activist tactics for their communication campaigns, facilitated communication and served as a crossroads for subcultures. Platoon was the name of the agency. Back then they mainly worked on labor union campaigns like the call for a minimum wage act, demanding 8.50 Euros per hour. In 2015, our efforts did bear fruit and with the help of lobbying, an official minimum wage was finally introduced in Germany. It is much higher now, I should add. Figuring out how to create political pressure by telling stories of people who suffer from our system, have a low-paying job and consequently live on the fringes of society, was a gripping project. The stories were meant to set the stage for debates. We had to figure out how to present them in such a way that they spark discussions and connect with society on an emotional level. Making sure people understood that this was hitting closer to home than they might have thought, especially when some of them were not affected by it directly.

K S Did it start out as an internship?

J K Exactly. I did an internship and ended up staying for a few additional years. Right before that, I had actually done another internship, in New York this time. I worked at a distributor of independent films by and about women. There, I was part of the editorial team and was responsible for cutting a film about the feminist writer Kathy Acker. The company still exists, it is called Women Make Movies. They started out in 1969. Since the film industry is traditionally extremely male-dominated, they have found their niche by exclusively supporting female directors and producers. Since then, they have become more open and diverse and support all people from marginalized groups such as the LGBTQI+, women with disabilities and women of color. Working in such a progressive feminist team has left a lasting impression on me.

After that, I went to Berlin because everyone said Berlin was so much cooler than New York. I thought to myself, well, you could check it out. One thing was certain, Berlin was much cheaper than New York. "Poor but sexy" is what Berlin's former Mayor Klaus Wowereit called it back then.

K S Is this when you started working for Platoon? I do not know if the word ideology fits but Platoon has always consisted of a team that tinkers with the world.

J K I used to work a lot in production, mostly producing videos and editing them. Storytelling and video cutting started to catch my attention relatively early on. Eventually I got tired of producing and really wanted to have a go at conceptualizing a more theoretical baseline. Thus, Utrecht in the Netherlands it was. I did a one-year Master's in New Media and Digital Culture, which focused precisely on the research of societal versus media theoretical frameworks as a means to understand the impact of media on humanity. The whole time, I was like a kid in a candy store because it was right down my alley. It was in English, it was abroad, it answered so many of my questions and helped me get my foot in the door in academia.

After graduating, I returned to Berlin. The program required me to do one

Fig. 2: At the SUPERRR office

final thing that I dreaded: a mandatory internship. While I struggled to come to terms with the purpose of it all, I decided to accept my fate and make the best of it. To network as efficiently as I could, I split the internship between three different companies. In one fell swoop, I managed to meet and connect with an overwhelming number of people. It was amazing!

One of the companies I interned at was Netzpolitik.org, which is still one of the most accredited blogs about digital politics. Then there was the Open Knowledge Foundation, which at the time worked a lot on transparency and open data. The last one is called Liquid Democracy. Their focal point was and is to this day digital democracy. They were all so different from each other, it felt like three completely different internships.

Open Knowledge Foundation granted me a project budget for the first idea I tackled, so of course I stayed. I managed to land my pitch and get the founder, who was in the UK, on board. My plan was to announce a competition relating to civil tech and call for submissions. A way of experimenting with digital technology to better public services and benefit civil society. City, Country, Code, that was the name of the project. Not only was it exciting to work on but it really took off. Many colleagues from the University of Applied Sciences in Graz actually helped me with the implementation.

One of them was Hellmut Monz. He produced the video. A good friend of mine who happens to be a journalist recorded the text. Tapping into our network of former fellow students was great!

While working on the project, I developed a bit of a liking for starting a business on my own. Thinking about how to hit your targets with one successful project in such a way that allows spin-offs is just the next logical step. Experiencing how it feels when someone trusts you to handle a project from start to finish, including keeping an eye on the budget and finances, was incredible. I was on a roll! I had the wind in my sails! This is the story of how I got into founding startups, fundraising and project management.

K S Your world today still revolves around that, is that right?

J K   Yes, it does. Circling around, identifying topics that do not get a lot of attention and new ideas and ways to convince others of them. In my case, those are philanthropic foundations I am trying to organize and plan budgets for that allow them to carry out said ideas. Ultimately, this is classic non-profit fundraising. However, we are constantly looking for new content, links and connections that have not been discovered yet. Not to mention hunting down interesting collaborative partnerships that qualify.

Over time, the projects have grown. Around 25,000 Euros were assigned to my first project. Generally speaking, for an intern, that was not bad at all. It goes hand in hand with responsibility. Eventually, you get to a point where you do not know if you can manage it all by yourself anymore.

My last and biggest project at the Open Knowledge Foundation was endowed with roughly 20 million Euros. 16 million Euros was given to non-profit projects working with open-source software. As you can see, the context has not changed much. We are still trying to design alternatives to the current digital technologies that corporations use to market and sell their products. Those alternatives are supposed to focus on the common good. Under the umbrella of this substantial project, we have been able to support a bunch of other smaller ones. And no, not every single one of their key features has to be directly linked to the main project. Once everything comes to an end, we always need to be able to show scientific proof and studies to define our output and draw conclusions, especially since we handle large sums of money. Despite all of this bureaucracy, it is cardinal that we do not neglect engaging people to set foot in new areas where they can explore, possibly grow and establish themselves. Programs like these are the ones I am most involved with. Not only the successful implementation of a project is of interest to me, but the creation of what I like to refer to as an entire ecosystem surrounding these projects.

> "When I entered the professional world, the consensus in digital politics was very much *anti*. Digital civil society organizations were against *surveillance, big tech* and of course *invasion of privacy*."

All of these are undoubtedly crucial topics we need to address. Among all of this negativity, there was I, interested in spotting potential for innovation, development and future visions. I was more concerned with the question of where and how to stand up for something instead of just standing up against it? For diversity, for security, for dialogue. I was looking a lot into government transparency. Brainstorming the positive impact on cities when citizens are given access to open data, brought me back to digital democracy. I believe it is possible to strengthen democracy and improve life in cities on all kinds of levels. We just need to ask the right questions. Free knowledge is definitely

something worth standing up for and contemplating its uses. There is a long list of places that could adopt this concept. For instance, museums and cultural institutions could open their archives, political processes could be more transparent, and companies could implement open software licenses to make codes publicly available in order to further develop them. I saw a lot of potential in sharing knowledge. Wondering how to make it all accessible, in the best way possible, was the next step.

What my team and I are currently working on is again something that is heavily leaning on optimism. We have noticed that civil-society organizations in particular are occupied with minimizing and averting damage. This is evident in many areas. Take the climate crisis for instance. Activists are protesting in the hopes of minimizing destruction.

Focusing on averting crisis leads us to lose track of the bigger picture, the actual goal. We cannot see the forest for the trees anymore. The sheer number of actual visible problems, like climate change, wars and questioning democracy is just too overwhelming at times. In our hasty world, we do not make time anymore to imagine what the future could look like in 20 years or so, mostly because it is exhausting, and we have forgotten how to do it. Most of us cannot fathom reimagining our health care and educational systems. We are wistful of the past and stuck in our status quo. This is another kind of crisis. An invisible one. What ends up happening is that we leave it to businesses like big corporations which in turn are spectacular at it. Their motivation is to hit revenue targets. They have no other choice but to become experts in the sales of tomorrow and the days after tomorrow. If we do not take initiative, we will be trapped in these narratives that are indoctrinated by businesses and politics. Politics are caught up in a similar crisis, which

JULIA KLOIBER

Fig. 3: Moderating In The Mean Time with guests Jillian York and Geraldine de Bastion at the re:publica conference, 2021, Berlin

affects us all but some more than others. They cannot imagine new ideas that would lead a way out. Networking and talking to people who do not share the same opinions as we do would be a first step in combating this issue. We are so comfortable in our bubbles that it has become too frightening to burst them.

K S And you do all this as part of your organization?

J K   Yes, as part of SUPERRR Lab, a non-profit company that I founded together with a former colleague of mine. Unlike an association with members and a board of directors, our structure is not enforced, light and flexible. At SUPERRR, we are two managing directors and a team of ten people. We started five years ago and have grown steadily since then, even though growth is not our primary focus.

From a feminist perspective, we home in on collaboration more so than growth, because we believe that is more sustainable. Granted it is distributed evenly amongst several organizations. I believe that if we set expansion as a goal, we could be bigger. With this approach, within five years, we could maybe be a team of 50 people. Now, we ensure a friendly partnership and cooperation with similar organizations that we share values and methods with.

That is exactly what eggs us on. How does one change systems or policies? What kind of stakeholder networks would one need for this? This requires ample competence and different skill sets, which often cannot be united under one single organization. Let me explain this using labor conditions in content moderation on social media—a topic we are currently engaged in. The conditions in this industry are borderline precarious. The content moderators are tasked with blocking illegal and violent content on platforms like Facebook and Instagram. For the sake of improving their health and safety at work, it entails labor lawyers, trade unions, investigative journalists, the workers themselves, politicians, authorities and without a doubt, the support of the public.

We are desperate for a civil society like ours that tends to persevere and leave no stone unturned. With employees being gutsy enough to come forward and congregate, we can corroborate their stories in support of change. Pertaining to advocating for and passing laws in addition to negotiating better policies, politicians are the crux of the matter politically speaking, while authorities take over safeguarding these regulations, checking they are being followed, on an executive level.

As you can see, there are a myriad of players that have to be considered. What I am wondering is, how to best group them together to get the ball rolling.

Is it possible to work it all out by yourself within one company if you have 150 people at your disposal that can take on these roles? Probably. Is it going to be rewarding at the end of the day? I doubt it. This would promote falling back into old patterns and we would be back to square one. Accepting multeity is the way to go. Giving these various groups the freedom to exist unlocks great potential. We then have to figure out how to facilitate dialogue between those groups. Networking trumps homogeneity.

"We do not function alone either. We got a *whole web of other companies* around us."

When there are 50 people on your payroll, you do have to come up with projects in order to finance them all. Having said that, our expenditure is never that great that we feel rushed to apply for 20 projects annually come hell or high water. This gives us the autonomy to choose our own projects carefully, picking those where we believe we can have some sort of impact. Circling back to focusing on collaboration instead of growth, this is just one of the many benefits of our philosophy.

K S I am curious to what extent politicians listen to you and your team?

J K   Although Berlin is certainly an important political powerhouse whose decisions influence Europe, never underestimate the impact of change on a local level. Local governments are more relatable since they have a direct impact on people's everyday lives. We have actual proof to show regarding your question. Some of our demands on feminist digital politics from last year are now part of the coalition agreement. I am on the advisory council responsible for the execution of the digital strategy. Sure, these are just the first steps, but getting this far alone is an amazing achievement. Now it is on us to implement and carry out our stipulations.

K S Are there any current projects concerning local politics?

J K   It is just a question of what to do first. In a local context, we have realized there is a lot more to do. Our office is in Kreuzberg, Berlin. Right in front of our door, there are problems and challenges that are in desperate need of attention. Tackling these issues is something we have slowly started to work on with local organizations. At the moment we are trying to figure out the starting point of it all while keeping in mind a better concept for the future.

Future Literacy for Civil Society is the name of this program. In total, we have 14 institutions—AIDS-Hilfe, a coworking space called BIWOC*Raising, an organization that fights for the rights of sex workers and organizations that focus on digital politics. This diversity allows us to come at it from a multitude of directions. Apart from local projects, we have to bring about change in the federal government, too. To accomplish this, we have to successfully convey and be able to pitch the content, use and usefulness of digital strategies for Germany with the intention of connecting all this with people's day-to-day lives. They need to understand that digital politics are also social politics in the sense that they are determined by similar topics like allocation, collaboration and sustainability.

Currently, digital politics are associated with economics, but it is a profoundly social and sociopolitical issue. We put our mind to it and made it our business to make sure this definition is the one that sticks. Teaming up with political parties, politicians and people in the administration that are open to such approaches is the sine qua non to get this motion rolling. Networking in the traditional sense is a huge part of it but there is a lot of work to be done outside politics. The fact that it is about the people themselves, the ones who work and have established careers in the ministries is thought too little of. Getting them on board, communicating with them is extremely valuable. We launched Feminist Tech Nights as a means of networking with them. They come over, share their progress on certain projects with us and in return get a chance to properly talk to one another since their offices and departments are super isolated from each other. Every one of them works in a kind of vacuum. As an NGO your top convincing argument will always have to be added value. Find a niche you can improve. Even though, sure, the world would be a better place without these gaps. At least we are trying to mend them.

Persistency is the key to change though. Sometimes it takes years of repeating the same thing over and over again. Which brings us back to storytelling. You have to be able to get your message across in a memorable and relatable manner. The audience needs to be able to retell the story as well. You rely on word of mouth if you want to be heard. Oftentimes you are reaching a level of abstract when speaking about technology, it is too hard for people to relate; it scares them away and you lose them. On top of that, most of them experience a form of sensory overload due to the constant exposure of the news and media every single day. Just adding to the noise does not always help. So how do you formulate a story that arouses curiosity and keeps them engaged and motivates them to get involved, participate? In a democracy it is important to mobilize individuals. It never has to be the majority of people, mostly because drawing in the majority for projects affecting marginalized groups is a contradiction in itself. As long as you have a bunch of smaller projects attracting different people, boom, you caught someone's attention. For them, seeing a direct effect of their participation is immensely empowering. We are an organization for the people, for society and generating interest, support and a following validates our existence. This aids in appearing legitimate and being taken seriously when approaching politicians with an agenda.

A great example is artificial intelligence. I believe most of us have used an AI application by now. It is just so convenient. But the ones being discriminated against by AI or suffering the repercussions are the others, vulnerable communities, the ones we do not see if we do not find them.

> "I believe most of us have used an *AI application* by now. It is just so convenient. But the ones being discriminated against by AI or suffering the repercussions are the others, *vulnerable communities*, the ones we do not see if we do not want to find them."

For recruiters, it has become common practice to use these tools. They are hardly ever up front about it. Trust me when I tell you that even you might have fallen victim to AI's obscurity in a recruitment process. Knowing they are employing AI tools that were trained on data including pseudo-scientific personality evaluations and tests to analyze your facial expressions for instance is infuriating. These data sets should never be employed in this kind of professional setting where they hold the power to decide whether you get promoted or hired. This decision ultimately has a huge impact on someone's life and whether they can pay their bills or not. Examples like these amplify just how important it is to fight for more transparency and educate people about the dangers and responsible use of AI.

This does not only affect people who live on the margins of society or do not have enough say or experience limitations of their rights. It can happen to almost

Fig. 4: Keynote speech at the transform_d Summit, 2023, Berlin

anyone. Stories like these are powerful in generating support for a certain cause.

K S Can you name and describe a favorite project from the last few years that illustrates your work well?

J K I would have to go back to content moderation and its horrid working conditions. Artificial Intelligence is the buzzword of the year. Effects and advantages of AI in general and in areas that will completely be revolutionized for the better—or not—thanks to this new technology are the center of attention. A lot of it is just hot air. Also known as good marketing. When things like AI come into the public eye, we cannot help but wonder how these things managed to pop out of nowhere. I want to lift that veil of secrecy and show the immense labor behind it, including the instability and dangers many of those workers face. We are blind to exploitation and injustice, especially in the production process, that make digital systems possible. In this context, I am currently looking at the new Supply Chain Act in the European Union. I want to know exactly what the supply chain looks like. Therefore, we are in close contact with workers in Kenya to investigate and shed light on potential human rights violations.

Digitization, digitalization and the digital transformation does not stop at national borders. You always have to look at things from a global perspective. Corporations and conglomerates are international. What kind of policies can be changed on a European, and even further, on a global scale to eradicate exploitation along the supply network for technologies like AI.

We work with employees and laborers who start labor councils and trade unions. Picturing those workers in a less secure and precarious work environment, most people automatically assume they are illiterate or are not qualified enough for a better job. In content moderation, it is de

Fig. 5

facto quite the opposite though. A large number of those employees have a master's degree or are simultaneously working on their PhD. So many of them have moved to Germany for their studies. Lacking adequate language skills for other jobs here, they started out in this line of work and despite the shockingly low pay, they kind of got stuck there. This job is extremely harmful to their mental health—it breaks some of them completely. People who leave this job are traumatized. As blatant as it sounds, unfortunately this is the harsh truth. There is no adequate training or support provided by the companies.

Our task as an organization is to partner up with those labor councils and see how we can assist in creating more transparency and complement their work through pushing for better working conditions in politics. This is just such a hot topic right now, it is crazy exciting to be a part of this transformation, this change. An empirical analysis is needed. You have to break down the facts into their technological, social, ecological and economic aspects. Measures must be taken. Let those be things like filing for proposals regarding regulations, networking, investigative and educational groundwork.

K S When you look at the world, you try to paint a picture, and you analyze it. You come across so many problems, yet you seem very optimistic. How come?

J K Now we are definitely coming back to the starting point. There is simply too much pessimism. What are we really missing these days? Optimism. Cognitive science has proven that we as humans have a certain penchant for dystopia, drama and disaster. We tend to be more attracted to all things catastrophic. Look at science fiction videos. They captivate an audience much more by showing how the world will end

tomorrow instead of letting us anticipate and deliberate how it could be saved.

The lack of these narratives motivates me to figure out tools that allow us to come up with them within a network of people. Trying to identify and use abundance in general, determining where to interfere, and finding what it takes to reconsider the obsolete are all part of this discovery, our work. Especially since humans have the conservative tendency to preserve and hold onto things. Change is not always positive. Fear of change is real. We need to break this cycle. We have to stand up for change, giving it a makeover. We need to keep saying change is good and necessary. If we do not take matters into our own hands, someone else will and we will be at the mercy of it. We have to participate, we have to be a part of the plan, we have to vote, like in the upcoming EU elections right now for example.

K S That actually just answered my last question. I was wondering what you thought of the next steps in terms of change.

J K A very small step, that is for certain. Everyone should put their thinking cap on and identify an approachable person in their neighborhood or social circle, who definitely does not share the same political ideas and perspectives on society. Start a conversation with them. Talk with them for a bit longer than small talk lasts. We cannot run away and hide from conflict if we ever want to discover new things. Learning how to properly structure a good argument in order to get your point across is an essential life skill I would say. Stepping out of our comfort zone, getting in touch with completely different perceptions of the world, learning from each other and actively practicing tolerance is a growth mindset I can definitely get behind.

A conversation between Andy Kaltenbrunner & Karl Stocker

Commuter In A
Communicating World

ANDY KALTENBRUNNER, political and media scientist, was one of the leading political journalists and digital developers in Austria from the eighties onwards, contributing as political editor for the news magazine profil in the nineties. Since 2000, he has worked internationally as a media researcher and consultant. In 2005, he founded Medienhaus Wien, a media and journalism research company oriented towards the common good, with partners from science and practice. He has headed its programs alongside professorships and teaching assignments at several universities and further education academies in Europe and the United States of America. As a project manager at the Austrian Academy of Sciences, he has been investigating transformation and innovation in journalism and media policy fundamentals. In 1996, he started off as the initiator and developer of several training and further education programs for journalists and media managers especially in Austria, Germany and Spain. Since 2020, he has been promoting and supporting the conception of public funding for independent journalism and media startups.

K S **You have started out as a typical, classic journalist, working for the Arbeiter-Zeitung and profil. What sparked your interest in journalism?**

A K Unlike what many other journalists claim, I must admit that I was not born with a passion for it, nor did I see it as some kind of calling. However, I have always been curious and never shied away from a debate. Somehow, more by chance than intention, I ended up in journalism at quite a young age. I was still studying political science and pedagogy in Vienna. To make ends meet as a student, I worked as a social worker and covered the graveyard shift at a youth club on the outskirts of the city.

K S **So, how did you end up in this line of work?**

A K Purely by coincidence. I sent a letter to the ombudsperson at the newspaper the Arbeiter-Zeitung, pointing out factual mistakes in one of their articles about working students. They printed a correction and then asked me to start writing for them, initially to report on my work at the youth club in suburban Vienna and other social issues. That was in 1981. Since these topics were not always front-page material, I mostly ended up in the weekend editions. Two years later, they made me the editor-in-chief of this feuilletonistic weekend supplement—probably the youngest person in this position for an Austrian daily newspaper.

Every Friday, we also published a 16-page issue dedicated to only one weekly topic called Das Thema. That was one of my favorite projects. We were the only newspaper that bothered to print such long articles, interviews, and reports focused on a single theme.

K S **How did you manage to score this position as the editor-in-chief for this weekend volume?**

A K My predecessor mentored and recommended me for the position upon her retirement. The management probably thought they had hit the jackpot—I was

Fig. 1: Andy Kaltenbrunner in his office in Benissa, Spain, in 2022

talented but cheap. The newspaper was undergoing a transitional phase, selling copies with hundreds of thousands of daily readers. It belonged to the Austrian Social Democratic Party and was not necessarily run for profit but aimed at maintaining a balanced budget. However, the proceeds for party newspapers from the classified ads steadily decreased over the years. Their last decade had begun. Attempts by the next generation of journalists to turn the Arbeiter-Zeitung into an independent left-liberal newspaper were thwarted by the party apparatus.

Today, getting a foot in the door the way I did at a prestigious news outlet as a young journalist is almost unfathomable. In 1982 and 1985, the Federal Ministries of Science and Education and for Family Affairs handed me a National State Award for Journalism for a series I wrote on social issues—at an age when today's university graduates are just starting their careers in the editorial offices. I would be a fool to deny that winning prizes like these at such a young age did not motivate me to keep going as a journalist.

Toward the end of the eighties, the publisher of the political weekly magazine profil hired me as an editor for their politics desk. At the time, profil was the most important, critical, and investigative medium—the benchmark for independent journalism. This time I was the one who thought I hit the jackpot.

K S **What excited you about journalism?**

A K   The opportunities working for profil were amazing. I was able to get my hands on all kinds of projects—political reports, interviews, biographical pieces, and investigative journalism. Above all, I have to say, I always loved the dialogue aspect. The possibility of speaking with all kinds of very different people is something I am passionate about. This is how I bridge theory and practice. Scientific reports and empirical findings have always been essential in my research and work, just as important as actually showing up on-site and trying to paint the most accurate picture I could about people's lives and struggles.

More than three decades ago, journalists could already see and investigate logical starting points and possible endpoints of the growing migration movements. This is what humanizes the data we use in journalism and science.

As a journalist, you may also have the chance to meet kings, prime ministers, and top industrial managers as I sometimes did. While those events seem exciting on the surface, there often is not much to take away that goes deeper, to be honest. But they make great snapshots.

When I was a young reporter, I witnessed Saddam Hussein in a small office in Baghdad graciously accepting Iraqi gold jewelry as private funding for financing warfare. For two hours, I stood in front of an unleashed crowd next to Muammar al-Gaddafi shouting out his strange philosophy at the University of Benghazi. I even met Bill Clinton for small talk about the relationship between the United States and Austria during an intimate 20, maybe 30-minute meeting with a very small group of editors in the Oval Office.

And yet, there was little of real relevance to report. I have vivid memories of my trips to Japan. In the late eighties, I met the management of Mazda in their elegant teahouse, thanks to a Japanese friend from the former high nobility. It was a very unusual honor for a foreigner. We drank tea. While all of this was thrilling in the moment and on the surface, it offered less insight for a political scientist as one would imagine.

Shortly after meeting with the carmaker's board, I encountered this wonderful older woman in Hiroshima. For three days, we went on long walks and just talked. She shared that she was the only one in her family to survive the detonation of the nuclear bomb when she was a teenager, just 500 meters from her house. Her life story left a lasting impression on me. These were the narratives I was passionate about presenting.

So, go out there and seek conversations with people who share their problems and concerns with you. If you do not do this, you will never understand theoretical concepts taught at school. The university library and media newsrooms can be creative production environments, but the life that powers and sustains these places happens outside. As a journalist or a scientist, you have the privilege to meet the poor and the rich, the hot ones and the ones who are just full of hot air, the powerful and the powerless.

K S What role has university played in your life?

A K   My studies were heavily influenced by several professors. One was the leading political scientist Emmerich Tálos, who later supervised my dissertation. During my time at university, I was particularly interested in his perspective on the establishment of the welfare state and his critical reappraisal of the evolution of democracy versus the rise of fascism in Europe. Even when I started working for newspapers, I kept coming back to academia, teaching and participating in research projects.

Another key mentor for my thesis was Cheryl Benard, a sociologist who has been a pioneering figure in early feminist research and, at the same time, a bestselling author. She introduced me to the works of the Berkeley sociologist Erving Goffman. His studies of social interaction have received criticism as too practice-oriented and not academic enough in Europe, especially in Austria and Germany. I found Goffman's sociological understanding of interaction and how to observe it in practice aligned with my own perception of relevant research.

Today, many researchers question this approach. Can someone really just sit, engage in conversation, observe, listen, ask questions, have discussions with people who are not experts, and then declare this a central part of research? Is it possible to write a text for the social sciences that anyone with some interest can easily read and comprehend, and still call it scientific? Can empirical research exist without relying on correlation coefficients to calculate and validate findings?

So as not to be misunderstood, I love data. But I also want to see it come to life.

K S It seems like you have found your place between practice and theory. Would you agree?

A K   Yes, but it is challenging at times. I have learned to live with skepticism from certain colleagues who doubt whether someone with 20 years of applied experience is able to fully grasp scientific concepts or talk about theories and the history of ideas. On the other hand, some young aspiring journalists who attend my seminars are surprised that I am able to quickly write up a two-column article in newspaper-style or capture, cut, and edit news videos on my phone. To them, at first glance, I am just an aging professor with theory talk. The translation between theory and practice is still difficult in both directions.

Fig. 2: Jeff Jarvis and Andy Kaltenbrunner at Café Prückel in December 2023

K S After 20 years as a journalist, you went into media consultancy. With your immense expertise, you overlooked cross-media projects, strategies, and digital transformation of big media companies. Am I correct in assuming that digitization, especially, could not have been an easy task back then when it was still a fairly new development?

A K It was the mid-nineties, and some media professionals in Austria and Germany, including myself, thought that the World Wide Web could have great potential. It was no coincidence that these were often people with an interest in research, tech development, social science, and international comparative studies. However, most media managers thought that the internet was a passing fad, and many traditional print and television journalists were of the same opinion.

In a kind of partisan act, I self-funded and set up online platforms within our magazine group without approval from the German co-owners. At that time, internet usage was only two to three percent of the population. Despite this, we almost instantly attracted thousands of followers who regularly visited our page, especially our weekly live online interviews with experts from politics, economics, and the arts, which also integrated the audience.

COMMUTER IN A COMMUNICATING WORLD

"A few friends of mine and I founded the small research company *Medienhaus Wien* in 2005, which is more of an *agile network node*. We wanted to have a space where we could exchange ideas, work, and get together."

After the turn of the millennium, Austria's leading magazines merged and shifted focus, causing our once successful revolutionary projects to fade into irrelevance. When that happened though, I had already left the publisher. In Austria, belief in a digital future for the media significantly declined after the dot-com bubble burst. We could count on one hand the ones who remained committed to digitization and digitalization—they are still on it to this day. Gerlinde Hinterleitner and her team at the news outlet Der Standard were Austria's pioneers in online publishing in 1995. The Austrian public broadcaster ORF was also one of the early birds, thanks to the commitment of editor Franz Manola. In Vorarlberg, the Russmedia group stayed ahead of the curve in other Austrian regions because, in the nineties, their very young owner Eugen Russ believed and invested in digitization and digital transformation.

I have learnt that beyond a good budget, every innovation needs persuasive and courageous leaders. For too long, the majority of the German and Austrian media industry managers thought the internet was not worth the effort. In my role as an international consultant, I was able to witness the progress being made in other countries. Scandinavians were Europe's early adopters—The Swedish Bonnier Group, the Norwegian Schibsted Group, and the Danish Broadcasting Corporation have been regarded as a benchmark.

After the financial crisis in 2008, which hurt a lot of major media companies, numerous innovative journalistic online projects emerged on both national and hyperlocal levels in southern Europe. It was an explosion of creative destruction. Newly founded news platforms like El Diario and El Confidencial in Spain have been successful with their digital journalism and community building. In the United Kingdom, I found The Guardian's leap from a relatively insignificant daily national paper to one of the world's largest online news platforms extremely impressive, all while maintaining a high quality of journalistic work. The publisher, Alan Rusbridger, a prophet of digitalization and some of his team shared valuable insights with me over the years.

We liked to go into the most experimental European and American newsrooms to gain insights into the future of journalism. Two great researchers and friends, Klaus Meier from Germany and José Garcia Avilés from Spain, joined me in touring and carefully studying innovation developments in media houses over the years, aiming to turn practice into theory and vice versa.

As early as the nineties, Manuel Castells described the upheavals as "the rise of the network society." He predicted the impact of digitization, digitalization and globalization quite accurately. However, those who read and quoted Castells to media professionals at the time were often regarded as mad scientists rather than practical experts.

K S Where has your research brought you?

A K It has become more interdisciplinary. I admire the thinkers and writers who cross many boundaries, like historian Yuval Noah Harari and neuroscientist Eric Kandels. I focus on a better understanding of communication, new journalism, value chains, rapid changes in society, the development of technologies, and how politics shape public life. In essence, all this leads to prescriptive and critical thinking about how we can defend ourselves against enemies of open-minded societies and fight for an enlightened public sphere. In one of our current projects, we are conducting basic research into how journalistic innovations work in democracies—asking very practical questions about how they can be supported.

We always wanted to bring this global expertise and experience home to Austria. A few friends of mine and I founded the small research company Medienhaus Wien in 2005, which is more of an agile network node. We wanted to have a space where we could exchange ideas, work, and get together. Matthias Karmasin, the Director of the Institute for Comparative Media and Communication Studies of the Austrian Academy of Sciences and Dean at the University of Klagenfurt; Alfred J. Noll, an attorney for media and constitutional lawyer and honestly, more of a philosopher; Astrid Zimmermann, an experienced representative of journalism then, and now the ombudsperson at the Austrian press council; Daniela Kraus, a historian who also used to be a media developer and now is the general secretary for the traditional press club Concordia. In times of economic and political pressure, Concordia is doing an important job as a stronghold for free journalism. They were all part of our amazing founding team when we started 20 years ago with the usual self-exploitation of researchers and without public money.

K S What has been the agenda of the Medienhaus Wien?

A K Before we formally established the research company, we had some simple questions in our informal networks, such as how many working journalists there were in Austria and what kind of educational background they had. We had many visions, but little did we know how the journalistic profession would change at the turn of the millennium. What is their self-perception? What should they be learning? Almost simultaneously, but independently, the Federal Ministry of Science—with a then conservative minister under a right-wing government—and the mayor's office in Vienna—chaired by a social democrat—contacted me with questions about potential organizational structures and curricula for the education of journalists. Our development team came up with a concept and was able to present it independently of party politics. As a result, in 2003, the official diploma program Journalism and Media Management for a University of Applied Sciences in Vienna was created.

K S Right, I was actually a part of the development team here in Graz at JOANNEUM, the University of Applied Sciences. They also started introducing a program for journalistic studies. I was teaching a course on contemporary history for it.

A K Yes, exactly. Those were the first two official programs offering a degree of higher education in this field of study. To have this in Austria took until the twenty-first century. Since then, Medienhaus Wien has created several other courses for various universities and academies in different countries. There is the undergraduate program Film and TV Production in Vienna and a postgraduate one called International Media Innovation Management based in Berlin, with European university partners and the Poynter Institute in the United States. Leading this executive master program with students from a dozen countries was especially a pleasure. They had the opportunity to discuss future topics with top innovators at the Guardian, New York Times, El Mundo, Die Welt, Google, HuffPost and many more old and very new media companies. Our faculty included renowned innovation researchers such as Lucy Küng, Nic Newman, Gerhard Apfelthaler, Phil Meyer, and guru of digital journalism, Jeff Jarvis, in addition to practitioners such as Wolfgang Blau, Gerhard Zeiler, and many more. It was an intellectual delight. Those were the days when we relished distinguished debates about futuristic scenarios before the term innovation got thrown around as a generic buzzword. Listening to knowledgeable experts and being allowed to ask contradictory questions with humility is one of the elements that make our work particularly enjoyable.

Furthermore, the municipality Vienna had tasked us to plan and establish an independent platform for further education. In 2011, that resulted in the educational association fjum—forum for journalism and media. Today, it is an essential meeting point in this business. Committed networks of professionals are needed today more urgently than ever as advocates for independent journalism. Since 2019, we have helped to develop concrete subsidy programs from federal organizations and foundations in Austria and Germany to support the future of journalism, such as the funding program Wiener Medieninitiative, which has already financed several dozens of journalistic innovation projects and start-ups since 2020.

Fig. 3: Introductory lecture at the Austrian Academy of Sciences in May 2024

K S How much of your work impacts society?

A K   I think the greatest effect my work has had was empowering people. In 1996, an early project with a long-term impact was an editorial course in magazine journalism which only ran for three years. I established the program at the magazine profil with the support of many colleagues from a wide range of competing media outlets and university partners. Selecting from hundreds of applicants, the very intensive training program only accepted around 35 participants. Today, almost all these graduates have leading roles in the press and media. Not only did we encourage them to efficiently utilize their craft, but we also created a powerful generation able to critically self-reflect and discuss the values of independent journalism that were introduced in several editorial offices at the time. In the best case, shared ideas of social responsibility are still upheld there.

K S You could have just rested on your oars then, right? But you do not stop, you keep going!

A K   Yes, that is just my mentality, I guess. We often have to destroy our own comfortable structures in order to make room for something new, exciting and better. In 2024, an international team published the book Innovations in Journalism. It was the result of three years of theory and fieldwork by 24 researchers in five countries between the ages of 22 and 62. We still want to better understand those new agents of transformation in the field of communication, support those who want to put their talent to good use and spread the word about the goals of democratic politics for instance. We urgently need that. We see societies disintegrate as right-wing extremists—again—obtain the majority of votes in elections in many countries. Part of the reason this is happening is the lack of a common source for credible information and discussion. Societies are disintegrating and becoming radicalized. Merely accepting this and remaining dormant would mean resignation.

K S I have noticed you mention Spain a lot. Where does your affiliation come from?

A K   It is all thanks to my wife. In her childhood, she practically spent every summer in Spain. When our first daughter was born, we went on parental leave together and spent some months there. We formed many friendships and several professional connections. I started to notice how much more advanced some of them were, in terms of creativity and digitization, in comparison to Central Europe.

While in Spain, I was able to get in contact with a quite newly established university in the state of Valencia, the Miguel Hernández University in Elche with an ambitious contemporary journalism institute. They are super forward minded with an amazing infrastructure on a campus with hundreds of palm trees. Not to mention, it is an exceptional wine region with fantastic local cuisine, which of course helps regarding it as a second home.

K S So, have you been going back there for 20 years now?

A K   Exactly. I am a commuter. Two thirds of my time working was distributed between Austria and Spain with the remaining third spent anywhere in the world.

Luckily, a lot of classes and educational programs now have online alternatives. Speaking of our individual carbon footprint, this is great progress.

K S Is it possible to advance change through technology?

A K Of course! It depends on the social, political, and economic environment embedding this technology. Imagining a democracy in a world with the internet was fascinating. Now, we are hoping Berthold Brecht's radio theory can come to life. Let every receiver also be a transmitter—this is the core theory. This is how the idea of an egalitarian democracy can spread and how we can put the social back in social media. It is tragic then, looking at the example of Elon Musk and how he, as a right-wing extremist propagandist and gatekeeper of X, takes on the role of a radical fire accelerator for social calamities just because he can and kind of feels like it.

This shows us that technology is a mere tool which, depending on the context—good and bad—can definitely help amplify change. This is why discussions about ethics and regulations are so crucial. Although using technology undoubtedly facilitates research, production, and communication, it does not replace original thought processes and critical reflection. Not yet at least. Artificial intelligence might be able to take this task away from us. In situations like this, it is even more important to check who is going to program, use, and own it, along with the motives behind it. Regardless of Donald Trump or Elon Musk, I still hope we can use technology for the better and to improve our quality of life by letting it take on mundane tasks, streamlining our workload.

K S Like this interview! After this, I just press a button and an app transcribes it for me. Before that it always took me days to turn it into a written document or I had to pay someone to do it. Now, the software does it for me. They are steadily improving too. Certain programs now recognize a lot of accents and dialects even.

A K Yes. However, I still notice the difference in quality when these documents are proofread by a human being even if these applications keep getting better. I value the collaboration of shortening, tightening and editing. But I can definitely appreciate what technological progress has done for us in the academic community.

K S With your lateral thinking and less institutional projects and general work, you definitely seem to have a positive effect on politicians, influential people, and society. I mean, is there really more one could ask for?

A K I have to say, sometimes it is not all roses. The projects that have worked out are the ones that motivate and keep me going. In the end, I never had to fill any important—but possibly boring—formal position becoming successful. But after 30 years of tirelessly raising awareness, frustration sometimes arises. Particularly when I observe political developments like the current ones in my home country these days—clearly contradicting the principles of an open society.

K S I have noticed privileged people whining about how life was better in the good old days—empirically not correct—does neither impress, nor affect you at all. You are reflective and highly optimistic. So, to conclude this, I would like to ask a very personal question. Where does it all hail from? What is your family background?

A K I am a child born out of wedlock to a family of farm laborers in Lower

> "Change was in the air. When former chancellor *Bruno Kreisky's Austrian government* introduced *free textbooks* in schools in *1972*, it marked an action of symbolic significance to this day."

Austria. When my mother was 14, she had to seek work as a domestic worker on a farm. At 18, she was accepted to a training school for nurses. In her later career she became Head of Nursing in a big Viennese hospital. In the beginning though, her salary would only be enough for a shared room in a dorm. She was a single parent and there was simply no space for me. Hence, I spent a few years at my grandparents' in a small village. When I was in school in the big city, I started to notice many positive economic trends, typical for my boomer generation. My stepfamily in Vienna started out in a 60-square-meter apartment for seven people that soon turned into two affordable homes in one of Vienna's social housing complexes. I was the first person in my family who could go for a higher education. During my summer vacations in the little farming village my grandfather boasted about me as a curiosity. Suddenly, it was even doable to finance your studies by working part-time in the evenings. Change was in the air. When former chancellor Bruno Kreisky's Austrian government introduced free textbooks in schools in 1972, it marked an action of symbolic significance to this day.

Before, us kids from financially struggling families were given old, sometimes damaged ones. I was so excited to finally own so many books. My books! For the first time in my life, I needed to get a bookshelf. Things did further improve, and yet what some now call the good old days were, in fact, not better for the majority in Central Europe. In the media industry, we also hear romanticized versions of the past, and that journalism was more sophisticated a few decades earlier. I then implore them to review the archive and read out-loud the editorials from the fifties or sixties. Smarter, more open-minded, just overall better journalism? As if!

Of course, now again, we see far too often a part of society that is left behind. We have media platforms that do business in a factitious way with populist, sometimes extreme groups that sell and appeal to the lowest instincts in people. On the contrary, we need a society that is well informed and can genuinely discuss issues like inclusive educational institutions, a fair distribution of resources, and the climate catastrophe without denying it. This is a huge responsibility for the next generation. But as a kid from a simple family growing up in the poorer suburbs of Vienna, I am always impressed when I compare that with the lives of my kids and their peers. Many of them are very well educated, polyglots, observant and tolerant. We should help them as best as we can, empowering the vulnerable and embarking on a rocky journey into a better world. They are the ones who give me hope. Where would we be without it?

A conversation between Sigrid Bürstmayr & Bettina Gjecaj

Empowering Change Through *Design Education*

SIGRID BÜRSTMAYR, MAG. (FH), M.A., is a designer and teaches at JOANNEUM, the University of Applied Sciences in Graz, exhibition design and sustainable design. As in any other discipline, she considers design to have a responsibility to act sustainably—that is, in a way that makes ecological, social and economic sense.

BETTINA GJECAJ DIPL. ING. (FH), MA, works and teaches at JOANNEUM, the University of Applied Sciences in Graz. Her professional interests and skills include green and social marketing, campaigning, public relations, corporate social responsibility, and strategic communication management. She describes herself as a tireless, energetic, full-blooded communicator and concept developer.

(S)(B) **What inspired you to study green marketing and develop an interest in sustainability? Were there certain events or experiences in your life that sparked this interest?**

(B)(G) Being a real city kid from Graz, Austria's second largest city, I grew up in a part of the city that would probably be labeled a problematic district today. That means a high unemployment rate, a high proportion of migrants, few green spaces, several empty properties, and betting shops, instead of organic food shops.

My mother comes from the classic proletarian background in Graz, with my grandmother working in a factory and my grandfather as a steelworker. My paternal grandparents were immigrants from former Yugoslavia. My grandmother was a housewife with four children, while my grandfather was a goldsmith. They fled the Tito regime in the fifties, originally intending to move to Australia, where the government at the time offered new settlers a piece of land. However, due to delays in family reunification and job opportunities for my grandfather, Graz eventually became their new home.

My parents were very young when they became pregnant with me. At only 18 years old, my arrival fundamentally changed their lives. They moved into a one-bedroom flat with a shared toilet in the corridor and had to put their education on hold while searching for work. Of course, as a small child, I was not aware of our circumstances, but once I started school, I began to notice differences between my situation and that of my classmates. Visits to the homes of school friends revealed these disparities, from the food they ate and the furniture in their homes to the cars their parents drove and their holiday destinations.

Fig. 1: Design+Science Summer School

This immersion with other living standards was always ambiguous for me. On one hand, I longed to live with their quality of life, however, on the other hand, these impressions had an inspiring and motivating effect on me. They confronted me with the fundamental question of how I desired to live in the future. At the same time, I also sensed the gap between these worlds and took a liking to the idea of building bridges.

With a strong desire to express my creativity, I pursued training at the Higher Institute of Technical Education and later at the University of Applied Sciences, specializing in information design. My career then took me to the world of television, where I worked as an editor at the news outlet Süddeutsche Zeitung TV. In this position, I embraced my role by writing reports and presenting people and their stories. This experience eventually led me to the non-profit organization Caritas, where I worked for almost ten years in the communications department, striving to empower people in difficult situations and teach them to help themselves.

I graduated with a Master's Degree in Green Marketing, which encouraged me to take up the position of lecturer at JOANNEUM. Looking back, I realize that finding meaning in my work and collaborating with people has remained a core part of who I am. My ongoing drive to address challenges and seek solutions for a better future for others continues to be my greatest motivation.

B G How did you become aware of ecological sustainability?

S B   I grew up in a home that resembles a living museum, overflowing with an eclectic mix of collections, mostly second-hand and often very old. There were boxes of wrapping paper, like an archive of floral and geometric patterns, as well as small boxes and tins filled to the brim with rescued zippers and buttons from forgotten garments, waiting to be repurposed. I vividly recall meticulously sorting these buttons by color and size. They could have probably been used to identify the fashion trends of past decades. Even used screws, wooden wedges and cords had their designated places in the house. Nails were carefully extracted from old boards, straightened if possible, and stored for future use. This lifestyle taught me a deep appreciation for resourcefulness, and the importance of avoiding waste. However, I admit, there were times when wearing clothes previously used by my siblings and cousins felt quite challenging.

I grew up in a close-knit family on a farm with my paternal grandparents, parents and four siblings. Belonging to a village of only 3,000 inhabitants, the farm is somewhat secluded in the idyllic Alpine foothills and surrounded by orchards. It was a great feeling to walk around the house each morning, bowl in hand, picking fresh berries for my breakfast muesli straight from the bush, or harvesting cherries, plums, and apples fresh from the tree. The garden was like a little paradise, where my mum carefully planted, harvested, and saved seeds for the next year's crops. As a child, I learned to process food, turning apples into juice, cider, jam, marmalade, and even dried apple rings. Opening walnuts for hours on quiet evenings was also part of our routine. I felt a certain sense of independence, at least from supermarkets. However, in winter, it would sometimes be tiresome to have only a menu consisting mainly of potatoes, cabbages and apples, each grown in their season on the farm. Weather conditions often determined whether a planned day of swimming would become an urgent day of haymaking. Hail damage to the apples, frost-bitten apricot blossoms, or trees uprooted by storms illustrated the dependence on the climate. The small neighboring forest provided wood for minor building work on the farm as well as for heating the entire farmhouse. In winter, the bedrooms were only heated for a few hours before going to bed. Nevertheless, thick duvets, flannel bed linens, and long-sleeved pajamas provided pleasant warmth. In summer, the thick old walls kept the rooms wonderfully cool. Holidays were limited to a few days visiting relatives in neighboring towns. All the more exciting were the school field trips and the first experiences abroad, especially after my final high school exams. I am very grateful to have grown up in an environment characterized by collecting, sorting, repairing, and reusing. It not only opened my eyes to the potential in seemingly worthless things, but also significantly shaped my understanding of the circular economy. I now realize that it was the sum of many

small actions, including the influences of my education, conferences, and travels, which have shaped my values and interests. As in every other discipline, I also see design as a responsibility to act sustainably, that is, in an ecologically, socially and economically sensible manner.

S B With your background knowledge and experience, how can we as designers build bridges between different social groups? What strategies and approaches can we use to overcome our own social bubbles and create more inclusive designs?

B G   I truly believe that it is becoming increasingly essential to develop an awareness of our own position as designers. Understanding this personal bubble is crucial for addressing real and sustainable solutions. Thus, it is important to consider these relevant questions: How can we ensure that those who do not enjoy the same privileges are also empowered? What does sustainability mean in contexts where social challenges are prevalent? How can we foster meaningful discussions about sustainability that include people from different classes, migration backgrounds, or religions?

Fig. 2:
EU project SMOTIES,
town square Oberzeiring

to instigate a turnaround for our planet, starting with combating poverty, eliminating inequality, empowering women and transforming food and energy systems (CLUB OF ROME 2022, p. 35).

To address these global challenges effectively, interdisciplinary thinking is pivotal, surpassing solely technical specialization. Design degree programs should reflect this need by promoting greater interdisciplinary collaboration and incorporating diverse elements into the curricula. Additionally, students should be introduced to scientific methods more extensively, enabling them to integrate sustainable findings into their design processes. While interdisciplinarity focuses on scientific exchange, transdisciplinarity emphasizes the role of non-scientific factors in problem definition and solution, aiming for long-term cooperation.

It goes a step further by extending beyond the realm of pure science, highlighting the partnership between stakeholders from businesses, politics, or civil society. Clearly, another important aspect of this is interdisciplinary cooperation, which is urgently needed to translate social problems into scientific questions. Furthermore, both partners in cooperation must jointly define fundamental principles, standards, and guidelines to ensure effective participation. This requires an unbiased and respectful engagement from the outset, with neither partner assuming a position of superiority (GÜNTHER / HONEKAMP 2013, p. 33ff.).

The third important approach to overcoming one's own bubble is engagement. Specifically, the inclusion of users and stakeholders in the design process. Participatory processes are also closely linked to the concept of social design and encompass all scenarios where professional and aspiring designers work jointly together. "Participation can range from the

In this context, the three related design principles which stand out as particularly relevant are inter- or transdisciplinarity, cooperation, and participation. The issues designers face is becoming increasingly complex, particularly because global changes like climate change impact all divisions of society. Solutions now require a breadth of proficiency beyond the capabilities of individuals. Both now and in the future, a diverse mix of expertise is essential to open up access to the Global Knowledge Society. In this context, the Earth4All analysis provides valuable insights, outlining five solution scenarios superficial, manipulative involvement of consumers in product development to radical forms of political activism in the context of social and political issues" (HELD / JOOST / MAREIS 2014, p. 17).

A positive example of building bridges between different social groups is the European Union project SMOTIES, which we have been working on since 2020. This project aims to develop space and service solutions through the design of cultural and creative innovations in ten small and remote places in Europe. It is part of the Human Cities network, a platform dedicated to interdisciplinary exchange aimed at improving the quality of public spaces and stimulating innovative processes for social cohesion through participatory design. It is truly inspiring to witness the outcomes when organizations, universities, students, residents, and entire associations join forces to find solutions together. For instance, in Oberzeiring, Styria, the project addressed the desires and needs of the population for a marketplace that served as a quality space for social interaction. Among other things, a ride-sharing bench was created where people can wait for a lift, as well as temporary furniture and greenery on the market square.

S B Yes, I think this project in particular describes the social impact of design very aptly. But why are there so few projects like this? It upsets me that in 1972, the international report The Limits to Growth published by the Club of Rome described the logicality of a circular economy, also referred to as cradle-to-cradle. It took 20 more years to conclude the transition to a linear economy, known as take-make-waste. Following this insight, the 17 Sustainable Development Goals were only created in 2015 by the United Nations. In your opinion, why is there such a delay to implement these demands in academic teachings? How can we close the gap between knowledge and action in design theory?

B G That is an excellent question. In my opinion, universities need to take a good look at themselves. Unfortunately, there is still a lack of a clear commitment to taking on genuine social responsibility. Holistic design education cannot be developed in a secluded department but must be integrated into the overarching framework of a university. This means that diversity management should be implemented not just at the micro level of individual courses but also at the meso level of curriculum design (AUFERKORTE-MICHAELIS / LINDE 2018, p. 100).

This also involves embracing diversity within universities—including demographic, cognitive, disciplinary, institutional, functional, and communicative structure for corporate culture diversity. The prerequisite for this is that educators are properly trained in these areas so they can impart this knowledge to their students (GAISCH / AICHINGER 2016, p. 6). While this holistic approach should already be a standard practice in all universities, it is evident that there is still significant progress to be made.

In addition to the question of attitude, I also think it is very important to empower teachers more with regard to ethical and moral decisions. Ethics, like the aforementioned topics, should become an integral part of the curriculum for aspiring designers to foster and enhance critical thinking skills. Design professor Christian Bauer criticizes the current lack of professional ethics training, which would help designers in making concrete decisions regarding economic and moral issues in connection with scientific and

> "Holistic design education cannot be developed in a *secluded department* but must be integrated into the *overarching framework* of a university."

technological advancement (BAUER 2022, p. 15ff.).

The modern world is characterized by VUCA, volatility, uncertainty, complexity, and ambiguity, which not only influences the content of teaching at design universities, but also the nature of teaching itself. Against the backdrop of increasing global, international, and interdisciplinary interrelations, the communication of values and knowledge structures plays an important role and looks at a variety of perceptual perspectives, prediction models, learning approaches, ways of thinking, problem-solving strategies and models of information processing. Universities that effectively leverage these cognitive and value-based differences as resources have a competitive advantage in terms of innovation, creativity, learning, and problem-solving-oriented action (AUFERKORTE-MICHAELIS / LINDE 2018, p. 110).

One possible solution to developing a concept for teaching is using the method of Education for Sustainable Development, which refers to a holistic and transformative education that takes into account learning content and outcomes, pedagogy and the learning environment. It aims to promote research-based, action-oriented and transformative learning through interactive teaching (BOHRMANN / DE HAAN 2008, p. 30). These are my thoughts on how to finally get this development moving!

B G Even as a small child, you were automatically drawn to the topic of ecological sustainability. In your opinion, how well do designers today fulfill their ecological responsibility?

S B   I realize that there is a lot of literature, research results, goals and reforms aimed at achieving a more ecologically sustainable way of life. And this is encouraging, specifically given our critical situation with climate change, resource depletion, poverty, and discrimination. We need change. However, much of this remains theoretical, and implementation often proceeds slowly. As previously mentioned, there is a gap between knowledge and action. The call for a transformation towards a post-growth society, where sustainable practices are prioritized, is growing stronger. This adaptation requires a radical change in both mindset and action. A shift from partially selfish, human-centered developments to environmentally friendly, planet-focused actions must be prioritized.

Fig. 3: Exhibition of the EU project SMOTIES

During my design studies, I was introduced to the concept of the cradle-to-cradle economy, with the fantastic prospect of an abundant supply of resources and the perpetual reuse of materials. 20 years later, I still have to explain the biological and technological circular economy to students in my teaching. I emphasize the importance of making crucial decisions at the start of every project. Decisions that not only extend the life cycle of products but also slow down the cycle in order to conserve resources.

For 150 years, design, among other industries, has both exacerbated today's resource shortages and contributed to environmental pollution. The consumer society, overproduction, economic growth, and the linear economic model are increasingly being scrutinized. Now is the time to take responsibility and solve the problems (BÖNINGER / FRENKLER / SCHMIDHUBER 2021, p. 253ff.).

The need for designers to take responsibility has long been recognized. As early as 1971, Victor Papanek wrote a kind of manual for human ecology and social change in his publication, Design for the Real World. He argued that "design must be an innovative, highly creative, cross-disciplinary tool responsive to the needs of men. It must be more research-oriented, and we must stop defiling the Earth itself with poorly designed objects and structures." (PAPANEK 2019, p. X). Papanek also states that, in an age of mass production, designers hold great power, as everything is designed and has an impact on the environment, society, and us. "This demands high social and moral responsibility from the designer." (PAPANEK 2019, p. IX).
This responsibility is even more urgent today, as each year sets new records for resource consumption. We need a societal and cultural transformation, from a culture of excess to a culture of moderation. Planning with a focus on elimination, omission, and reduction is goal-oriented design (cf. WELZER 2013). The principle of less but better has been an important philosophy for decades, and relates to both the consumer society, as well as ethics and values. "You cannot understand good design if you do not understand people: design is made for people." (RAMS 1976).

B G I see it the same way. How do you think we can bring this more than urgent transformation to the design universities?

S B   I am convinced that specialized bachelor's or master's degree programs, such as Eco Design, Social Design, or Sustainable Design, should eventually become unnecessary. Instead, the principles of sustainable design should be integrated into every design discipline, whether web, graphic, product, media, sound, or exhibition design. Sustainability must no longer be an elective or supplementary subject, instead a fundamental aspect of every design course. Ecological, social, and economic considerations must bolster all design projects.

However, there is still much work to be done before we reach this goal. According to the Future of Design Education Initiative, many university design programs continue to predominantly focus on the external appearance of objects. Meanwhile, job opportunities in this area are dwindling, while the social and technical impact of the digital revolution is increasing and the environmental impact is growing (FUTURE OF DESIGN EDUCATION 2024).

I also see critical thinking as a central element in design education. Firstly, to enable and encourage students to judiciously evaluate briefings, goals, and data we need to motivate them to think outside the box and prepare them for unforeseen challenges in the future. Secondly, students must develop the ability to analytically self-reflect, scrutinize their own ideas and projects, test, and revise them. Cultivating critical thinking takes time and a lot of space.

As an example from my teaching activities, I would like to mention the Design+Science Summer School. The focus here is on interdisciplinary work, time for discussion, future-oriented topics and exploratory outcomes (DESIGN+SCIENCE SUMMER SCHOOL 2024).

The Tongji University paper, Sustainability in the Future of Design Education, describes the following topics for a contemporary design curriculum: Fundamentals of Sustainability, Circular Economy, Whole System Thinking, Impact, Assessment, Laws and Standards, Communication, Collaboration and Leadership (ACAROGLU / COOPER / GARDIEN / FALUDI / PAPELA / SUMTER 2023, pp. 163ff.). One approach of Teresa Franqueira, international coordinator of the DESIS—Design for Social Innovation and Sustainability—Network is to promote a new generation of design activists who bring about change through their work. The world is changing and with it the role of the designer and the tasks of design education (WDO 2024).

B G Yes, and finally I conclude that until recently, people were at the center of design, but we have long since arrived at the next stage, namely planet-centric design, which promotes the equal treatment of human and non-human stakeholders and stresses dynamic interrelationships in ecosystems. "Cross-functional multidisciplinary teams now develop products, services and systems. The age of the solo designer is mostly over." This is one of the most important messages for the design theory of the future (DAVIS / DUBBERLY 2023, p. 102).

As designers, we should always ask ourselves the question posed by design theorist Tony Fry, "Do the things we create justify the things we destroy?" (FRY 2008, p. 4f). Sustainable design decisions should always address this important question. Moreover, we should structure our entire curriculum according to the idea of science theorist Donna Haraway, as expressed in her book Staying with the Trouble. This means remaining faithful to the problematic conditions, constantly approaching, and exposing ourselves to them anew (HARAWAY 2016).

REFERENCES

ACAROGLU / COOPER / GARDIEN / FALUDI / PAPELA / SUMTER 2023 = Acaroglu, Leyla/ Cooper, Cindy/ Gardien, Paul/ Faludi, Jeremy/ Papela, Ana/ Sumter, Deborah (2023) Sustainability in the Future of Design Education, Amsterdam: Hogeschool van Amsterdam

AUFERKORTE-MICHALIS / LINDE 2018 = Auferkorte-Michalis, Nicole/ Linde, Frank (2018) Diversity Teaching and Learning. A university textbook. Leverkusen: Budrich

BAUER 2022 = Bauer, Christian (2022) Ethics for designers, Stuttgart: avedition

BOHRMANN / DE HAAN 2008 = Bohrmann, Inka/ De Haan, Gerhard (2008) Competences in Education for Sustainable Development. Operationalisation, measurement, framework conditions, findings. Berlin, Heidelberg, New York: Springer-Verlag

BÖNINGER / FRENKLER / SCHMIDHUBER 2021 = Böninger, Christoph/ Frenkler, Fritz/ Schmidhuber, Susanne (2021) Designing Design Education. White paper on the future of design education. Stuttgart: avEdition 2021

CLUB OF ROME 2022 = CLUB OF ROME (2022) Earth For All - a survival guide for our planet. Munich: Oekom

DAVIS / DUBBERLY 2023 = Davis, Meredith/ Dubberly, Hugh (2023) Rethinking Design Education, Tongji University

DESIGN+SCIENCE SUMMER SCHOOL 2024 = www.designscience.school, University of Ljubljana, University of Split, FH JOANNEUM, PiNA [22/07/2024]

FRY 2008 = Fry, Tony (2008) Design Futuring: Sustainability, Ethics and New Practice. Oxford: Berg Publishers

FUTURE OF DESIGN EDUCATION 2024 = www.futureofdesigneducation.org/ [22/07/2024]

GAISCH / AICHINGER 2016 = Gaisch, Martina/ Aichinger, Regina (2016) Das Diversity Wheel der FH OÖ: Wie die Umsetzung einer ganzheitlichen Diversitätskultur an der Fachhochschule gelingen kann - 10. Forschungsforum der Österreichischen Fachhochschulen, Vienna: FFH Forum

GÜNTHER / HONEKAMP 2013 = Günther, Anja/ Honekamp, Wilfried (2013) Interdisciplinary teaching. HDS. Journal - Perspectives on good teaching. Leipzig: Hochschuldidaktik Sachsen

HARAWAY 2016 = Haraway, Donna J. (2016) Staying with the Trouble, Making Kin in the Chthulucene. North Yorkshire: Duke University Press

HELD / JOOST / MAREIS 2014 = Held, Matthias/ Joost, Gesche/ Mareis, Claudia (2014) Wer gestaltet die Gestaltung? Practice, theory and history of participatory design. Bielefeld: Transcript

PAPANEK 2019 = Papanek, Victor (2019) Design for the Real World. London: Thames & Hudson

RAMS 1976 = Rams, Dieter (1976) Speech in Jack Lenor Larsen's New York showroom: Design by Vitsœ

WDO 2024 = Franqueira, Teresa (2021) Defining Design Activis: www.design-activism-with-teresa-franqueira/ [22/07/2024]

WELZER 2013 = Harald Welzer (2013) Transformation Design. How to get to a sustainable modernity (and how not to), lecture at GLOBArt Academy, www.youtube.com/watch?v=HyWUS-dvfVg [22/07/2024]

A conversation between John Howkins & Christina Hedin

Curiosity And *Creativity*

JOHN HOWKINS is an analyst and author whose books describe major changes in the way we think and work. The common theme is creativity and innovation. His book The Creative Economy is the standard text on creative industries. John is both an entrepreneur, a co-founder and chair of several startups and a visiting professor at two universities. John has worked with a wide range of organizations in over 30 countries to increase understanding and innovation in a business environment.

C H You have explored the concept of creativity for a long time. What have you discovered?

J H Well, that is a big question. When I first began writing about creativity, I focused on the creative industries and the creative economy—on the people whose work relies on it. I noticed that these industries had many similarities, and I wanted to understand what connected them.

Initially, I described the scale of what they were doing, and the numbers of people involved. And I became increasingly interested in the individuals themselves. Over time, my focus shifted to understanding their motivation, what influences them, and their emotions and thought processes, as opposed to just looking at the end result.

I found that there was little scientific consensus on the circumstances, inspiration, or indeed the purpose of creativity. The method was very murky. It was mysterious. For centuries, creativity has been thought to be a divine gift. It had to be original in the sense of being new and different, but that was the only requirement. This raises the question of who judges novelty and difference and by what criteria.

Back then, we did not have the tools to look inside the brain or understand mental processes. But as neuroimaging and data analysis technologies developed towards the turn of the twentieth century, scientists began to have the technical means to do precise neuroimaging and large-scale data analysis. Today, the neuroscience of creativity is almost entirely focused on these questions of process rather than on the output.

We still struggle to define outcomes such as art or design satisfactorily. Everyone has their own idea of what these terms mean, but we have no clear scientific definition of art. In fact, as we gain more insights into the creative process, we lose some of the old certainties about art. In the past, people talked about a canon of literature and music, but now the term is highly contested. My current focus is almost entirely on the process of creativity, from individual motivation onward.

Previously, we would identify something as an artwork, a design, a building or fashion and label it as being creative. By default, for lack of knowing what was actually happening, we assumed the process, whatever it was, was creative. I call this working backwards.

Nowadays, we understand more about why people pursue creativity. Whether in designing clothes or buildings, we can identify key elements of the process

Fig. 1: During many years, John Howkins has been traveling to China and built up a large network of colleagues and friends.

like motivations, ideas, and techniques, even if the final result does not make these obvious. Taking that into account, we can actually identify them, even if the work is not finished. I call this working forwards.

Perhaps the most significant insight is the role of the individual. The origins of creativity are personal and often private, tied to how individuals perceive their identity, and make a mark on the future. Creativity becomes a way of asserting oneself and making a unique contribution to one's identity, rather than simply following in the footsteps of previous generations.

I am looking around the world and I am having ideas. Looking at omnipresent concepts from different perspectives, trying to shake things up and arrive at new concepts which I hope interest other people. Through that process, I will change, and they will change, and it is a dynamic and transformational cycle.

Not only do people become architects in order to create beautiful buildings. They do it because it generates a strong feeling of contentment. Designing involves a myriad of tasks, from mapping out plans to making decisions and adding personal touches, which makes the process enjoyable and fulfilling, even if it is difficult.

C H What keeps it interesting to develop this subject?

J H   The ongoing puzzle of defining creativity. Since I have been focusing on the creative economy for the past 20 years, I know that a definitive answer to what constitutes creativity remains elusive. So, I thought, why not try to work out what it is myself. And that has been going on for two or three years now.

Ever since the emergence of generative artificial intelligence, such as ChatGPT, people have been wondering whether this technology is actually creating something.

This is a really important question. So far, creativity as we practice it, has always been regarded as a supreme achievement of humankind that differentiates us from other animals. However, artificial intelligence has managed to mimic us with unerring accuracy. We as humanity do need to cross-examine the originality of those creations.

Yet, we cannot properly start this debate until we have worked out what creativity is and what it means. Only then will we be able to differentiate between our own and a machine's and identify areas where they indeed overlap.

Knowing this will allow us to instill more confidence in our own creativity, which in return will assist in learning how to make the most of this technology. At the moment, filmmakers and fashion designers are very keen on using artificial intelligence. They think it is wonderful, and they want to incorporate it everywhere due to the fact that it increases their efficiency and productivity. Many mainstream businesses share the same approach. Conversely, the majority of writers are terrified of it, and do not like the idea that this application is easily able to produce a 70,000-word novel almost instantaneously. This is their bread and butter. Of course they are worried and upset.

Taking a closer look at the tension and fretfulness, you will notice it is about so much more than just a bunch of stories written by a machine. At root, we are losing something believed to be a uniquely human quality. This ability to envision and imagine, creating art and culture as well as thinking up new tools is now being mirrored by a device we invented in the first place. Long have we thought of the achievements in poetry, music, art and architecture as something distinctly human. For a long time, these glories of our civilization had always separated us from other animals.

Michelangelo, Bach and Beethoven, Picasso and van Gogh, Newton and Einstein—anyone who is thought to be creative, even a genius, has always been accepted as being the same species as the rest of us. We simply could not conjure up the image of any other animal or machine showing the same creative traits. Especially one that was invented by us!

C H Is creativity a way to develop the world and can it make the world a better place?

J H   I do think so, yes. Of course, it can be used to come up with some ideas that are very damaging to other people, either immediately or in the long term. But in general, people want to be creative because they want to add something positive and transformative to the world. Take Picasso for example. He created paintings and drawings that he felt should be made. He wanted to push the boundaries, showing society what could be done. In his world, he was making art that he believed was essential, but that only he could make it. Naturally, many people disagreed, including plenty of painters.

Nobody is creative unless they really want to be. In a way, this can be quite selfish. You cannot order someone or instruct them to be creative. Being motivated by a feeling of pure bliss and enjoyment, people will only do it if they want to. For some, it is a middling, easy pleasure. For some, an intense, overwhelming passion.

I am not saying they are philanthropists, as they are not necessarily doing it to be kind to other people. They are longing for a world that is more to their liking. This is what drives them.

Making an effort in this sense is looked at as worthwhile because they want to produce something that did not exist before. They are contributing to the variety of life in a way that they think is important. When we say creativity makes the world a better place, we are referring to this ambition, this motivation, this desire.

It is not merely making something faster or cheaper but forming something transcendental and changing people's perceptions. We also obtain pleasure when we express our creativity.

C H What is the most important thing about creativity you have learnt this year?

J H   I have been reading some articles by Blaise Agüera y Arcas about a Spanish neuroscientist called Santiago Ramón y Cajal. Ramón's pioneering images of brain networks are still used today. He was the first to show, from the eighteen-eighties onwards, that the brain is not a single unit but rather a network of cells with varying connections with other cells.

I went on to read what else Agüera had written. He is wonderfully perceptive about AI and lots of other things. He is half-Spanish but was born in New York and brought up in Mexico and became a tech entrepreneur. He is now a Senior Fellow at Google and an author and one of those rare people who understand artificial intelligence from the inside, as it were, but also understand the historical context. I mean, about our relationship with machines and, one of his big concerns, how we create and extend our personal identity.

Through him, I have learnt about the amazing similarity between perception and creativity. This had not occurred to me before, but now seems very basic. It works like this. The brain processes how we perceive what already exists and how we create new ideas in the same way, although of course in different directions. We look around and try to make sense of what is out there, so to speak, so that we

> "Nobody is creative unless they really want to be. In a way, this can be quite *selfish*. You cannot *order* someone or *instruct* them to be creative."

can classify it and remember it. We cannot remember things unless we can classify them and label them, which is why we cannot remember dreams or fantasies, or seemingly inexplicable and shocking events. Then, when we try to make something new, we gather a bundle of memories and put something out there for others to interpret.

What we make for others to see may be exactly the same as what we perceived previously, or we can filter and transform our memories in some way.

How we do so depends on our physical make-up, our culture, our personal circumstances and our sense of identity. It depends on our motivations, desires, likes and dislikes and so on. It depends on whether we are with others who are also thinking along the same lines, or maybe who disagree with us. It is at these moments that we can be creative.

This is my main discovery this year and it has changed how I think about creativity. I have also discovered that separate research shows how memories are organized to help us play around and do things differently to how we did them before. It was long thought that the brain stored memories according to their content and importance to us. That is still true. But the brain evaluates their content and relevance in unexpected ways. Research by the Princeton Neurological Institute, PNI, at Princeton University shows that memories seem to be stored as much according to our circumstances at the time as by what we might see as their intrinsic relevance. So, thoughts and memories of something said in a particular room will be stored together with others that happened in that room, as well as their intrinsic relevance. Of course, we do not know this. We are not in control of how our memories organize things. PNI refers to so-called meaning spaces, which are like little boxes of memories with all kinds of different associations.

And there is another line of research. This shows the importance of someone's personal view of the world, their own place in it, and even more notably, what they want their place to be in the future. This involves their personhood and identity and their motivation to change things and make their own mark on the world.

These three discoveries, each made by different researchers in different areas of neuroscience, allow us to make a map of how creativity actually operates. This is the first time it has been possible. It is directly relevant to education and how we learn. It affects our understanding of aesthetics. I think it also has a bearing on business management.

Fig. 2: John Howkins at second World Cultural Capitals: Tianfu Symposium, Chengdu 2019

Most important is that it affects how we might devise new, creative solutions for the global problems that threaten our survival: climate change, poverty, dictators, and conflict. By creative, I mean solutions that are new, elegant and useful.

This research also informs our understanding of artificial intelligence. The similarity of perception and creativity has been supported by research into the neural networks used in large language models. Google research shows that perception and creativity are mathematically very similar. You can run the same algorithms to process both, albeit in different directions.

There is another benefit. We already know a lot about perception and how it works. Even better, people love talking about it. We love doing tests like the black-and-white images that could be either a candlestick or two people's faces in profile. In fact, of course, it is both. Playing around with what we can see is the basis of many children's games as well as magic, the circus and fancy dress. People are often embarrassed to talk about their own creativity, but they love talking about their perception.

C H **For many years, you have been collaborating with China. What can you tell us about their development since you first arrived?**

J H We have to realize that China had more people than anyone else in the world for many centuries. At one point, it was the richest country in the world. We tend to think of old China as being poor and deprived. This was not the case at all. Up to about 1500, it was a hotspot for technological inventions. For many years, China was highly advanced.

And then, from about 1750 onward, it closed down. So did Japan and Korea. This all happened right when the Industrial

Revolution started in Europe and the United States. In due course, China and large parts of Asia were scarcely touched by the European enlightenment and scientific revolution. Had they not shut down, it would have affected them since the main European countries were or had been colonial powers. Industrial innovation spread around the world at warp speed on the grounds of this.

China's rulers have often battled to unify its territory. Even before now, past dynasties have already been concerned about protecting their landmass and defining borders. It never really had a colonial mindset, and rarely made its way to other countries for the benefits of trade.

C H **What brought you to China?**

J H Curiosity. The same curiosity that drives most of my life. I read about the Cultural Revolution and the death of Mao in 1976, and I could not understand it. I was ignorant of what was really happening, but I was reading the headlines, and I thought, this was extraordinary. At that time, I was working as a journalist, specializing in global communications. Despite never having been to China, or not knowing much about it, I felt an urge to go there.

It took about two years to organize the trip. As a solo traveler, it was very difficult to enter the country. In 1979, I finally made it and returned a few times in the early eighties. In the nineties, I was even able to work in Beijing for a few months. By 2006, I was traveling there on a regular basis. In Shanghai, a research center on creative economy was established in my name. The government there wanted to know about copyright and intellectual property in general, but particularly copyright. Intrigued by the creative economy, they came to me. As an insider, they quizzed me on what was driving Western creativity.

C H **Have you ever been an expert in China's creative economy?**

J H I had a front row seat at China's modernization in arts, culture, design, and media. I was very lucky and privileged.

About six times a year, I went to many different cities, teaching businesses, local governments, universities, entrepreneurs and party officials. Inevitably, I was able to get extraordinary insight into what they were thinking, how they went about the shift to modernism, and how they viewed innovation.

First of all, they were interested in how to run a business that depends on creativity, how to boost it, manage talent, and reflect it in the products. I gave a lot of fairly straightforward entrepreneurial advice on understanding markets and setting prices.

One line of interest was how to live and how to work in order to maximize creativity, contemplating whether we should all come together in a type of creativity hub. Shanghai alone set up about 80 of those. While some of them were successful, others did not work out—for good reasons. No matter the outcome, they all sent a strong message showing the government's support and appreciation of creativity.

Next off, they wanted to study how to design a city that encouraged and inspired originality and inventiveness. Chinese officials and architects traveled a bunch and visited places like New York, Milan, London, Los Angeles, San Francisco, and Seattle. They examined these creative nuclei, trying to figure out how to establish this back home. By dint of them vigorously collecting inspiration, I became involved in plenty of master planning and urban design projects.

Since 1949, the state has owned most of the land. In practice, that means various levels of government have predominant control. The municipality in

Fig. 3: Chengdu 2019

Shanghai provides leases for periods of about 50 to 70 years. The proprietorship of real estate and plots of land is a major source of wealth and income. As the economy prospers, property becomes more valuable. The government can lease more sites to a developer. Having this much say and control enables the government to allocate grounds for specific uses such as housing, roads, hospitals, schools, creative hubs, and so on at any point in time. If necessary, they will also contribute to their construction. In Europe, it is very different.

I became involved in working with local governments, property developers as well as companies representing industries that were in need of space for new locations. Typically, these were businesses that would benefit from being in a so-called creative park, like the film production and games industry or really any company specializing in design or animation.

Moreover, I became involved in China's development of intellectual property. There is a general rule that countries do not pay much attention to trademarks and patents when it concerns their import. Once they start exporting them, all of a sudden, they do start to matter. America ignored all of this when it imported books and paintings from Europe and was therefore the world's biggest infringer of European copyright. Only when it began to export its own films and TV did it become relevant. Similarly, China only began to worry about patents when it started to export them.

In all this, I provided a mix of technical and business advice. I described how copyright, patents, and design rights operate, analyzing the international market as a whole, as well as looking at effective and successful venture outlines.

Above all, I was giving people the confidence to do it and do it really well. Not

Fig. 4: World Cities Culture Forum, Chengdu 2023

just in their own neighborhood or country but perhaps in a way that would enable them to export. At this level, being creative in any field is very competitive.

When I talk to people in China and America, it is clear that they have a lot in common. Software engineers and game developers apply the same techniques and skills, in addition to often working with similar hardware and software packages. They are learning from their peers and noticing what is being done elsewhere. They do communicate with each other, they participate in the global market, buy foreign brands and travel. There is a lot of exchange going on and even if that just means visiting a festival in a different country.

Of course, the extent of it always depends on the occupational and cultural sector you are referring to. There is less mingling and intertwining when it comes to more traditional and language-based fields such as most theater and traditional music. Most of the time, they are tailored to a local audience so much so that, internationally speaking, they do not translate well. In contrast, branches that are non-verbal, such as architecture and design, are universal and spark global conversations.

C H **The past years, you have been writing a great number of books. As of yet, how many have there been in total?**

J H I wrote a lot on all kinds of topics while working at the International Institute of Communications. There were books on satellites, which were reshaping international communications, then some about television broadcasting, new electronic media and the internet as well as communications in Finland. My first visit to China in 1979 was financed by my book

192

called Mass Communication in China. It was the first time a foreigner had written about this topic while actually using interviews with locals. I was delighted to see it was still on the reading list at Peking University over 20 years later.

In 2001, I published The Creative Economy, which was revised in 2006 and again in 2013. Fortunately, it came out right at a time when people were heavily into learning about the creative economy and wanted to get down to the nitty-gritty of it. It has become the most read of all my publications and has led to my work in China and to nearly all my work at the moment.

Creative Ecology was issued in 2019. It originated from a Chinese project led by the state council which wanted to adjust the school curriculum, making sure it prepared teenagers for the world in which they would soon be working. The council asked the Shanghai government, plus five or six universities, to describe how the future would look in ten years from then. We spent about a year coming up with different scenarios. Afterwards, the University of Queensland in Australia offered to publish my contribution in their new series on the creative economy and innovation.

C H Do you have any trips planned, or any projects in the offing?

J H   The World Conference on the Creative Economy in Uzbekistan in October of this year is on my itinerary. This is a major biannual event that, with the support of the United Nations, commenced in Indonesia. There is an Executive MBA I have been teaching at Hong Kong University that hopefully I will be returning to also.

My travels, though, have certainly declined since COVID restrictions. Climate change dampens my enthusiasm for travel too. Before, all we had to think about was whether our schedule would make it possible and if it was interesting enough. Now, the main question we ask is about necessity. I miss traveling. I studied international relations at university and have often worked with companies that were operating on a global scale. I now long for this kind of networking, exchanging ideas and making new friends.

C H Do you have hope for the world for the upcoming years?

J H   Hope? Is that a word that comes easily when one discusses the future of the world? I am not sure. It is not the first word that comes to mind. I hope that Joe Biden wins the US election, although I think it is unlikely. I hope we do not have any major climate catastrophe, but it seems likely we will. And I hope we do not suffer any serious AI malfunctions.

The world is increasingly interconnected and very fragile. We see the rise of autocrats with the resources and skills to act in their own selfish interests with a corresponding decline in the international order and institutions.

I suppose my hope is that the world prevails until we can find ways of solving these dreadful problems of poverty, war and climate change. Restraining the growing number of autocrats that seem increasingly uncontrollable is unavoidable if we want to achieve any of this. They seem to be finding more and more ways of gaining control and staying in power regardless of what is good for their populations. I do not see that changing anytime soon.

I hope a multiplicity of small initiatives will gradually help to mitigate the problems and that we carry on until then.

We must not get discouraged by a sense of hopelessness. Staying cheerful and determined to think positively, I think that is important.

A conversation between Carlotta Beghi & Christina Hedin

Youth Involvement *As A Catalyst For Change*

CARLOTTA BEGHI is the Focal Point for Parma, a UNESCO Creative City of Gastronomy. A 2015 graduate with a Master's degree in Communication, Organization and Marketing of Territorial Food and Wine from the University of Parma, she has followed the project since its candidacy. Her experience, which began at a young age, drives her goal to involve the younger generation in creating change. "Invest in the potential of youth skills, and watch the world transform into a masterpiece."

C H **What role does your passion for Parma play in your desire to contribute to the City of Gastronomy?**

C B   When I am asked to contribute to a publication like this, I often feel puzzled. I do not see myself as an expert on the subject, I simply approach my work with passion, striving to create something meaningful. When I was invited to share my personal perspective on the City of Gastronomy, my story and thoughts, I decided to focus on my own experiences. My inspiration for anything professional, Henri Poincaré, said, "Creativity is combining existing elements with new connections that are useful." This encapsulates my journey of making the change that I intend to present.

This experience of mine began in March 2014 when I earned my degree in Public Relations and Advertising in Milan, a complex city, which offers multiple opportunities, yet its fast-paced lifestyle did not align with my vision of life. Returning to Parma was the goal. While it is a small city, sometimes too small, Parma is my city, my place, the land that I cherish. Living there, I strive to look beyond its boundaries, refusing to let the physical limits make my world feel too confined. Ultimately, my aim is to make useful contributions to the city I love so deeply.

C H **What motivated you to choose the internship at the City Council of Parma?**

C B   After a brief experience in the United States, I pursued a master's program focusing on local produce, framing the cultural background, and how to market it. This would certainly bring me back to the city. When it comes to gastronomy, it stands out as a reference point, offering an indisputable wealth of opportunities.

The master's program included a lecture period followed by a curricular internship, which would serve as the basis for my final project. I received two acceptance letters. One from a production facility of an excellent comestible and the other from the City Council of Parma.

I had to make a decision, as both places had accepted my application, and this choice would undoubtedly influence my immediate future. To this day, I sometimes wonder if I made the right choice. I was young, perhaps a bit naive. Eager to return home to be able to contribute to something meaningful because there is so much potential with incredible resources. Therefore, I felt compelled to put my all into elevating this region and all its wonderful attributes. To speak of valorization means considering it a living, complex reality that evolves and requires interpretation.

One of the two options seemed to me the easiest way to realize this ambition, so I began my internship at the City Council of Parma. I was fortunate enough to be assigned right away to the project of the city's candidacy as a UNESCO Creative City of Gastronomy.

In my position, I was lucky to work alongside people who believed in my abilities and placed their trust in me, choosing to invest in my professional development over the years; something that is far from guaranteed, so I feel very fortunate.

Especially when it comes to creative skills, which need to be constantly revised to remain relevant to the current cultural models and significant challenges in order to face and leverage the opportunities, which may come about, I learned how to apply those with respect to futures literacy.

More than anyone else, the coordinator of the master's program at that time, who guided me through this internship and later became a colleague and one of

Fig. 1: Parma, famous for the Parmigiano-Reggiano cheese

stayed and, today, I serve as the Focal Point of Parma. My work aligns perfectly with Poincaré's definition actually. It is perfect for me! Essentially, my role consists of seizing and creating opportunities to improve the region and support its residents.

We try to focus on fostering generative strategies and practices that are inclusive and responsive to drive change. In 2015, my then supervisor, now colleague, entrusted and supported me despite my inexperience. This has been my inspiration to do the same and engage young people in many of our current projects. I truly believe this is a key in turning any project into something wonderful!

> "Invest in the *potential of youth skills*, and watch the world transform into a *masterpiece*."

my dearest friends, truly believed in me and created opportunities for my growth.

Just three years my senior, she became both my role model and mentor. Sometimes, I do still wonder whether I made the right choice since municipal work is undeniably challenging. Yet, reflecting on her influence is what truly guides me every day as I strive to contribute to sustainable and valuable change.

C H What are your goals for the future of the Creative City and its young residents?

C B The candidacy I oversaw was successful, leading to Parma being designated a UNESCO Creative City in 2015. I

When people are exposed to exciting ideas and opportunities in addition to being handed the tools to be creative, they can tackle anything and everything. This represents the most immediate, effective, and sustainable investment for a prosperous future of our city.

The Creative City is a space for applying a future-oriented vision that recognizes young people as agents of change and social transformation. It is where we can cultivate opportunities that foster a creative milieu (LANDRY 2000) in which ideas can flow freely, thereby stimulating sustainable development.

By including the younger generations and providing educational opportunities, they receive first-hand experience and knowledge about sustainability and possible contributions to their communities. They develop awareness and become critical thinkers, while addressing global challenges. In this process, they can emerge as the change-makers, communicators, innovators and leaders of tomorrow.

I want them to thrive as individuals, to be heard and valued as social actors. Creating this environment and setting is essential for unlocking their potential and creativity. With all this talk of effectiveness and efficiency, I do not want them to be viewed as just a mundane workforce with an amazing skill set. My role is to culturally guide and empower them in order to assist in finding meaning and value in the world which hopefully influences the way they approach projects. This has been my focus for the past eight years and continues to be my mission.

C H How do you empower interns?

C B I host interns in our office for Food Policy and the UNESCO Creative City, where I enable and motivate them to come up with and tackle personal projects. This gives them the opportunity to learn, work, and participate in decisions that ultimately influence them. Additionally, I have been supervising University of Parma students in their dissertation.

I always respond with sincerity and passion to the questions of those entering the workforce, guided by the values and enthusiasm I had in 2015, and still possess to this day.

I have worked as a lecturer at the University of Parma, teaching courses on the UNESCO Creative City initiative and striving to convey a vision that nurtures creativity within the city.

I have also sent interns abroad to other Creative Cities to diversify and expand their knowledge. In line with that, I have coordinated European projects that facilitated the mobility of young people, allowing them to visit these cities and exchange ideas with their peers. My collaboration aimed at fostering their creativity is meant to help them fortify their role in society, redefine their profession, and grow an ever-widening sphere of influence.

Implementing this training and experience into their entrepreneurship later will lead to significant social transformation. This just demonstrates how gastronomy can be a powerful tool for change, as highlighted by the Basque Culinary World Prize.

Each of these small initiatives aims to nurture learning—an inherently creative act—and personal growth, enabling them to thrive, but also understand and exercise their rights. I would love to get them to a point where they turn into responsible innovators with an impeccable sense of community.

"Youth involvement in all its forms serves as a catalyst for change towards building a more inclusive and equitable world."

C H How do you involve young people in Parma with the work of UNESCO's Creative Cities of Gastronomy?

C B Similar to creating a dish, you combine existing elements to craft something new and see how the idea resonates. Many people are eager to discuss opportunities abroad, but we also need to focus on our local community.

I would love to get involved again with Erasmus+. We have regional funds for digital initiatives, and I am excited to use them for training courses and activities. Our university here consistently focuses on high-quality projects, which have been

Fig. 2: UNESCO workshop

a delight and I am planning to pursue this collaboration.

Before my maternity leave, I had three interns. One wrote a possible candidacy proposal from an Italian city to join the network, and it was amazing. Another intern traveled to Zhale, a UNESCO Creative City of Gastronomy in Lebanon, to prepare its UNESCO monitoring report. For this, I actually assisted the Focal Point there in finding an additional intern for the task, which turned out to be a super fun joint effort. The third intern followed a project involving young food creatives.

I tried to lead and manage these assignments so they would bring about valuable insights, along with a deeper understanding of international and national partnership and teamwork instead of simply handing them a vague roadmap that led to dispersed and scattered knowledge on how to organize events. Trying to teach them to see the bigger picture that links everyone and everything was important to me. I would love to do something similar again.

Another project I am working on with the university is a prize for the best thesis related to any UNESCO topic. Selecting the winner is going to be quite the challenge! I have identified all the courses, the PhDs and master's programs eligible for the award. We require them to major in topics related to gastronomy, sustainability, marketing, tourism, packaging or agriculture and their thesis to be connected to the 2030 Agenda, preferably MONDIACULT, the UNESCO World Conference on Cultural Policies and Sustainable Development. Recently, some sponsors decided that the prize-giving should be the main event of Parma as the Creative City of Gastronomy. We are excited to explore various topics and enhance our branding efforts. The prize money can be used for an

Fig. 3: UNESCO Creative City in collaboration with Erasmus+; a study tour program teaching about the local cuisine and produce in Parma

Fig. 4: Cheese production

internship, further studies, or however the recipient chooses.

Due to this prize, the jury is now forced to read the thesis in order to select the best one. The winner will have to present their work to the whole gastronomy community, which includes key figures and influential sponsors. And while personally, I find it daunting to publicly speak in front of such an important audience, it is an incredible opportunity.

Here, I can only stress the link between gastronomy and change again because it bears so much meaning for me. At the moment, I am heavily honing in on winter school, which will be a short university course on gastronomy aimed to offer quality insights about issues crucial to the development of future-proof, cultural cities, with a specific focus on food. The topics will be addressed through theoretical lectures and case studies framed in the context of the 2030 Agenda for Sustainable Development and the MONDIACULT Declaration. Through the winter school we aim to position Parma as an international platform for collaboration and dialogue on sustainable and regenerative city design.

We have secured the funds to kick this off and to have at least five scholarships! And I am dedicated to finding the right teachers for the program. Regardless of our limited budget, we have found some that expressed genuine interest. This is super encouraging to see! I truly appreciate our network of like-minded individuals.

C H What would you change if you could decide more in the city of gastronomy of Parma?

C B Increasing the funding of internship programs and scholarships in the interest of reaching more high school students and getting them on board would be one of the first things I would do. Not to say we have not collaborated with them in the past at all, just on a smaller scale than I think is needed to have a greater impact and really make the most of it. So far, we have organized discussions about Creative Cities and art workshops where they created paintings based on keywords prompted during brainstorming sessions, which were then showcased at exhibitions. It is so inspiring to see young teenagers embrace their creativity and remember the joy of childhood. I would love to further develop and expand those projects and opportunities.

Inviting one of those students to our UNESCO annual meetings where they can meet other people in my position from other cities and witness the interaction and exchange between us and politicians would be an amazing chance for everyone involved. For example, if that one student were a chef, it could be a top student from ALMA, The School of Italian Culinary Arts, joining us. However, I know that such opportunities are often hindered by power dynamics and jealousy among those in decision-making positions. If I were in charge, this would be another top priority for change.

The trick is to send the right people to those UNESCO events. Sometimes people or their superiors hesitate, which stops them to travel. Beforehand, a lot of them are not aware of the extraordinary potential that attending those events carries. Once you have been there, you understand the value it brings, which is why I am trying to make them progressively detect and appreciate those chances. People often say that it seems like I am going on a week-long vacation, but I am actually working towards bringing back possibilities for my city, not for myself.

Events we attend are selected carefully. Each trip offers unique learning opportunities and different goals. Whether it is to explore marketing strategies or to motivate students to attend our winter school program.

Right now, becoming the European Youth Capital is one thing we are trying to achieve. I believe several projects could truly flourish under this title, especially the initiative I envisioned with high schools and the Italian Youth Association for UNESCO. I am already seeking funding

> **i** THE CITY OF PARMA IS DESIGNATED AS A UNESCO CREATIVE CITY OF GASTRONOMY SINCE 2015.
>
> To get accepted as a Creative City, your city needs to see creativity as a driving force for urban development and implement it to achieve the 17 Sustainable Development Goals of the UN. There are seven different creative fields: music, literature, film, design, crafts and folk arts, media arts and gastronomy.

for this, but gaining the appellation would simplify the process and improve our chances. Introducing the issue of urban regeneration by combining it with food related topics as an extracurricular high school subject or event is just another impactful idea we would like to work on.

I love discussions with young people about their experience of the city through food and gastronomy. Not just about the products, recipes or the act of cooking. We talk about food in the way they share it on social media. While I do have to admit I might be too old and out of touch with their slang and culture—take my absence from TikTok as an example here—I am willing to try and give them a platform so we can bridge the generational gap and truly understand them and their needs so we can include and support them properly. Exploring their way of communication and creative use of tools has great potential for pushing forward innovative ideas in gastronomy and projects concerning our city.

C H **What would you say is the key to getting the youth involved in a good way?**

C B I need to think that through. A few years ago, for a Gola Gola festival in Parma, a celebration of food, art, and culture, we partnered with high schools. I held a one-hour lesson about Parma as a UNESCO Creative City of Gastronomy by explaining all the organizational details, using fun images and including quotes from people they know and could relate to. We divided them into groups and each of them was assigned a different topic. They discussed key phrases and words. After posting their ideas on the wall, they then had to paint or draw something based on their conversations. They did an amazing job, and I was mostly just there listening,

not inferring at all. By the end, everyone felt a sense of accomplishment and creativity as they admired their artwork.

They were given a voice and felt like they were a part of something incredible. Most of the time it can take a few moments before participants start to feel comfortable sharing their thoughts without fear of being ridiculed or saying something wrong. In my experience, especially with the project I just mentioned, there was simply no space for calling something wrong, we listened to everything they had to say. Support, validation and allowing freedom of speech is so important for any successful cooperation. Actually, I am convinced that stopping them after a less significant comment would have had the exact opposite effect to what we wanted to, and managed to, achieve. It would have smothered the whole process and limited their creativity. Engaging with the concept and finding their own path through trial and error is extremely paramount to their further development. We are providing the space for it to prosper. We collected a few ideas for future funds and tried to show them how much we genuinely care and want them involved. I am so glad we could do that. They expressed great interest in projects concerning urban regeneration and public art installation, so this is something we want to further explore now. Unless we start talking to them on a regular basis, their ideas will not be heard. Identifying locations and allocating a budget are the next steps we have to take in order to let this come to fruition.

People are leaving the city centers and moving further out because it is cheaper and—especially relevant after COVID—because housing with an attached garden is affordable and there are more open spaces. We have so many empty shops and buildings in the city center, so those could also be spaces for young people to use

> "I like to think of our job as *creating* or *spreading possibilities.* Spotting potential is something I am good at. Once I have found it, I will go out of my way to *incorporate those people into our projects.*"

creatively. In the UNESCO network I meet people from different places that are facing similar problems in their cities. There is a mutual understanding and in regard to this shared problem, I draw inspiration from those interactions. Since all of my efforts focus on long-term goals, I cherish the work with young people so much. It makes me happy when I see them believing in the things we are talking about.

We had an intern who wanted to learn how to organize events, so initially, we assigned her to this particular department. After showing up to and discussing with us at the open lab, she realized that she in fact did not want to pursue a career in event planning. Instead, she was now super intrigued by organizations like UNESCO and wanted to give it a try. We talked a bit more in detail about my job, I shared a few documents and after consideration, she has decided to study English this year and has made plans to enroll in a university program related to UNESCO cities in general and the design of those Creative Cities. Moments like these confirm my efforts to include young people.

Neither do I consider myself a creative person, nor do I excel in cooking or have extensive knowledge of nutrition or food. Yet, I am passionate about my role, and I strive to convey that enthusiasm because I truly believe it is valuable. If I can ignite interest and excitement in just one person for the work we do at UNESCO and inspire them to make their mark or have a positive impact on their city, then honestly, that is enough for me.

I like to think of our job as creating or spreading possibilities. Spotting potential is something I am good at. Once I have found it, I will go out of my way to incorporate those people into our projects. Unfortunately, not everyone here shares the same mindset and it can be hard and frustrating at times but it is undoubtedly worth the effort and something I stand for.

To be honest, people like you who believe in making a change and always try to get others involved, make me really love my job. Working with you opens my eyes to new possibilities, and that is exactly what makes this role so fulfilling.

List of Figures

STUART WALKER

Portrait	P.10	James Mackie
Fig. 1	P.14	Nikos Antzoulatos
Fig. 2	P.15	Design Commit
Fig. 3	P.16	Highwire
Fig. 4-8	P.18-19	Stuart Walker
Fig. 9	P.23	China Summit
Fig. 10	P.24	James Mackie

LILIÁN GONZÁLEZ-GONZÁLEZ

Portrait	P.26	Lilián González-González
Fig. 1-4	P.29-34	Lilián González-González

GUNNAR RUNDGREN

Portrait	P.38	Jens Lasthein
Fig. 1-5	P.41-50	Gunnar Rundgren

STELLA ROLLIG

Portrait	P.54	Gianmaria Gava / Belvedere, Wien
Fig. 1	P.56	Sandro Zanzinger / Belvedere, Wien
Fig. 2	P.58-59	Ingo Pertramer
Fig. 3	P.61	Johannes Stoll / Belvedere, Wien
Fig. 4	P.63	David Payr / Belvedere, Wien
Fig. 5-6	P.64-65	Ouriel Morgensztern

PIER PAOLO PERUCCIO

Portrait	P.66	World Design Organization
Fig. 1	P.69	World Design Organization
Fig. 2	P.70	Jose de la O
Fig. 3	P.73	Pier Paolo Peruccio
Fig. 4	P.75	Massimiliano Viglioglia

MARSHA MUSIC

Portrait	P.78	Bri Hayes courtesy detroit contemporary
Fig. 1	P.80	Marsha Music/Family Collection
Fig. 2	P.85	Stephen McGee
Fig. 3	P.86-87	Marsha Music/Family Collection
Fig. 4	P.88	Mary Ann Mangano
Fig. 5	P.93	Stephen McGee
Fig. 6	P.93	Cover photo by Jeff Cancelosi

LUKÁŠ BERBERICH

| Portrait | P.98 | Matúš Chovan/Kino Úsmev Archive |
| Fig. 1-6 | P.100-105 | Kino Úsmev Archive |

BARBARA MEYER

Portrait	P.106	Luis Krummenacher/S27
Fig. 1-6	P.109-117	Luis Krummenacher/S27
Fig. 7	P.119	Karl Stocker
Fig. 8-12	P.120-129	Luis Krummenacher/S27

OLA FRANSSON

| Portrait | P.130 | Ola Fransson |
| Fig. 1-3 | P.132-139 | Christina Hedin |

JULIA KLOIBNER

Portrait	P.142	Marlene Burz
Fig. 1	P.145	Stefanie Loos
Fig. 2	P.147	Ole Witt
Fig. 3	P.150-151	Gregor Fischer
Fig. 4	P.155	Christina Czybik & Laurin Schmid
Fig. 5	P.156	Marlene Burz

ANDY KALTENBRUNNER

Portrait	P.158	Carina Brunthaler
Fig. 1	P.160	Franz Suttner / Medienhaus Wien
Fig. 2-3	P.163-166	Medienhaus Wien

SIGRID BÜRSTMAYR, BETTINA GJECAJ

Portrait	P.170	Hannah Wasserfaller / FH JOANNEUM
Fig. 1	P.172	Tine Lisjak
Fig. 2-3	P.174-178	FH JOANNEUM

JOHN HOWKINS

| Portrait | P.182 | Christina Hedin |
| Fig. 1-4 | P.184-192 | Christina Hedin |

CARLOTTA BEGHI

| Portrait | P.195 | Christina Hedin |
| Fig. 1-4 | P.197-200 | Christina Hedin |

The Editors

Christina Hedin has dedicated her career to sustainability, environmental issues, and the development of local and organic food. She holds a B.Sc. in Environmental Science from Mid Sweden University, where she discovered and fell in love with the natural beauty of the surrounding mountains, forests, and lakes.

For 15 years, Christina worked at the Swedish National Centre for Artisan Food and spent five years contributing to the development of organic agriculture in Southeast Asia and East Africa. Her passion for sustainable food production has also taken her around the world through her involvement with the UNESCO Creative Cities Network. Since 2015, she has been an active member of the network and she has also spoken about sustainable food at UNESCO conferences in Paris, Beijing, Hui'an, Chengdu, Macao, Kanazawa, Östersund, Norrköping, and Graz.

Christina has been a local political leader in Östersund for 14 years and has now transitioned to the international stage, working at the EU Parliament in Brussels. She is passionate about combining her political work with her commitment to environmental sustainability and culinary culture.

Sophie Kauper left Germany and moved to Bangladesh in 2011. Working for Dipshikha, a local NGO that focuses on preventing rural flight, she documented and assessed existing conditions to improve projects that promote equal rights. Finding comfort in the unfamiliar, in 2013, she found work as an English teacher in Chengdu. After more than two years in China, followed by a brief stay in the United States, she relocated to Kingston, Jamaica, where she dedicated most of her time to rescuing stray dogs. Two years later, she enrolled in the Water Management and Environmental Engineering program at the University of Natural Resources and Life Sciences in Vienna. This allowed her to discover her love for geodesy, geology, and math. As a student, she joined the Office of Sustainable Development and Global South of the Austrian National Union of Students, organizing events and acting as a student representative in committees as well as the Equal Opportunities Working Party. She now lives in Graz, Austria, working as a freelance English teacher and math tutor, still devoting much of her time to animal welfare.

Karl Stocker is a historian, educator, researcher and consultant in culture & design, an author and editor of books and scientific contributions. His professional and academic interests include design & theory, design & society, exhibition design and socio & sustainable design. For 30 years, he has directed and curated exhibitions and contributed numerous projects to other exhibits. He was Head of the Design and Communication Institute at the University of Applied Sciences in Graz for many years. He was a professor at the University of Kassel from 1996 to 1997, Visiting Professor at the Berlin University of the Arts from 2009 to 2015, and since 1988 he has been a professor at the University of Graz. Since October 2024, he has served as the Head of the English-language PhD program in Media Arts and Digital Media at Tbilisi State Academy of Arts.

Editors: Christina Hedin, SE-Östersund, Sophie Kauper and Karl Stocker, AT-Graz

Translation: Sophie Kauper, AT-Graz and Lauren Brooks, JM-Kingston
Copy Editing: Sophie Kauper, AT-Graz and Lauren Brooks, JM-Kingston
Proofreading: Sophie Kauper, AT-Graz and Lauren Brooks, JM-Kingston
Cover and Graphic Design: Kerstin Harrer, Lukas Huber, AT-Vienna

On behalf of the publisher
Acquisitions Editor: David Marold
Content Editor: Angelika Gaal
Production Editor: Heike Strempel-Bevacqua

Printing and Binding: Gugler Medien GmbH, AT-Melk
Printed in Austria

Paper: Pergraphica Natural Rough FSC Mix Credit 120 g/m²

Library of Congress Control Number: 2025934571
Bibliographic information published by the German National Library
The German National Library lists this publication in the Deutsche Nationalbibliografie; detailed bibliographic data are available on the Internet at http://dnb.dnb.de.

This work is subject to copyright. All rights are reserved, whether the whole or part of the material is concerned, specifically the rights of translation, reprinting, re-use of illustrations, recitation, broadcasting, reproduction on microfilms or in other ways, and storage in databases. For any kind of use, permission of the copyright owner must be obtained.

ISBN 978-3-0356-2980-4
e-ISBN (PDF) 978-3-0356-2981-1

© 2025 Birkhäuser Verlag GmbH, Basel
Im Westfeld 8, 4055 Basel, Switzerland
Part of Walter de Gruyter GmbH, Berlin/Boston

www.birkhauser.com
Questions about General Product Safety Regulation productsafety@degruyterbrill.com

9 8 7 6 5 4 3 2 1